MASSINAHIGAN SERIES

Brief Accounts of Early Native America

Vol. 5

"You have your Massinahigan*; (that is to say, you have a knowledge of writing), which makes you remember everything."*

—An Algonquin captain to Champlain at Quebec, 1633. The *Jesuit Relations*, Vol. 5, p. 207.

The Roman Rite
in the
Algonquian and Iroquoian
Missions

From the Colonial Period to the
Second Vatican Council

Claudio R. Salvucci

Evolution Publishing
Merchantville, NJ
2008

©2008 by Evolution Publishing
Merchantville, New Jersey.

First Edition

ISBN 978-1-889758-89-3

Library of Congress Cataloging-in-Publication Data

Salvucci, Claudio R.
  The Roman rite in the Algonquian and Iroquoian missions : from
the colonial period to the Second Vatican Council / Claudio R.
Salvucci. ~ 1st ed.
      p. cm. ~ (Massinahigan series ; v. 5)
  Includes bibliographical references and index.
  ISBN 978-1-889758-89-3
  1. Algonquian Indians~Missions~History. 2. Iroquoian Indians~
Missions~History. 3. Algonquian Indians~Religion. 4. Iroquoian
Indians~Religion. 5.   Catholic Church~Missions~East (U.S.)~
History. 6. Catholic Church~Liturgy. I. Title.
  E99.A35S35 2008
  973.04'973~dc22

                                        2008026432

Table of Contents

List of illustrations

Acknowledgements

I am indebted to my good friend John Rotondi, who provided invaluable perspective and shared his seemingly inexhaustible knowledge of the historical and liturgical intricacies of the classical Roman Rite, and to Karl Tricomi, whose musical wisdom and extensive experience gave me a much better grasp of the music of the traditional Mass.

Also worthy of special mention are Father James McLucas, who kindly published some of my initial research on the Algonquian and Iroquoian liturgies in *Latin Mass Magazine*. Shawn Tribe encouraged my studies and offered incalculable assistance not only in matters liturgical but also in referring me to scholars in the field. I am especially indebted to Dom Alcuin Reid for his time and his sage insights. Father Raymond Bucko and Father Carl Starkloff provided me much-needed anthropological context and kindly corrected some of my brash overstatements and insaccuracies. And especially dear to me personally were the contributions of Teresa Sappier and James Sappier, who offered their personal memories of the Masses at Old Town.

I could not have even conceived of such a work without two tremendous and devoted priests of the Holy Roman Church, whose zeal for preserving its ancient traditions in the midst of indifference and hostility invites no small comparison with the great Indian missionaries of old. My dear friend Father John A. Perricone's intense and infectious love for the Holy Sacrifice was my first significant exposure to classical liturgy and had no small impact on my own appreciation for it. And I owe so very much to my indefatigable pastor Father Robert C. Pasley, KHS, under whose spiritual care I have been entrusted for the last few years. Even years of library research and interviews with renowned experts could never have replaced their contributions to this book—as they taught me the traditional Roman liturgy not merely as a historical artifact to be dissected and analyzed but as a spiritual discipline to be lived.

Finally, there is no one on earth of whom I am more appreciative for her constant support than my dear wife Jamie, who endured my strange obsessions and academic distractions with good humor, and my son Benjamin, whose pending arrival was my impetus to at last put this research into publishable form.

+ Preface +

To date there has not been a great deal of scholarly interest taken in the distinctive traditions that grew up around the Catholic Indian missions of North America. The history of these localities seems to garner some interest, but if the residents' religious practices are sometimes studied, they tend to be broadly considered as interesting anthropological cases of the encounter between the Catholic religion and Eastern Woodland culture—where they are often completely mischaracterized as "syncretism", a term which really should be used of religions that only borrow certain elements of Christianity, remain outside the visible Church, and do not concern themselves with orthodoxy.

This work, however, concerns itself with neither the history or the anthropology of the Eastern Woodland missions, but rather their liturgical practices as compared to the rest of Catholic Christianity. It intends to treat the usages of such places as Kahnawake or Oka in the same way we are accustomed to hear about, say, the Use of Sarum or the Ambrosian or Mozarabic Rites.

To my knowledge, such a thing has never been done. And the reason for this, in modern times at any rate, is probably the very distorted picture we have inherited of Native American Catholicism. Modern commentators within the Catholic fold as well as outside it sometimes seem to work under an assumption that the Church before the Second Vatican Council enforced a kind of ecclesiastical imperialism to which those Indians who accepted Baptism were expected to absolutely conform.

But an examination of the evidence shows that the Catholic Church from the 1600s to the late 1800s was quite often the preserver and sanctifier—not the destroyer—of native culture.

Whatever political, social, and ecological turmoil that raged around them, the mission towns spoke their own languages at home and had a rare privilege to sing them at Mass, in many cases continuing their cultures and their domestic arts almost completely intact. For over 300 years, towns like Kahnawake, Akwesasne, Odanak, and Lorette boasted devoted congregations of Catholics, who throughout these centuries have made particular local contributions to the Church universal. But for the practice of Christianity, their residents differed not very greatly from their pagan countrymen.

In the late 1800s and the early 1900s however, there seems to have been something of a shift in ecclesiastical tolerance of such communities. Many Catholic prelates of North America, taking a cue from the general American spirit of the time, saw in the native way of life a doomed and useless vestige of a bygone era. Well-meaning ecclesiastics then began to make a concerted effort to eradicate the "Indianness" of the mission towns and to encourage them to conform in culture, behavior, and language to the Anglo-Saxons around them, in very much the same way as was expected of the new European immigrants off the boat.

Without questioning the motives of these pious individuals or their judgment, it is safe to say the passage of time has proven them entirely wrong. The Indian mission towns even a century later are still very much intact and alive, and the assault against native culture did not achieve its intended assimilationist victory. In fact, it generated a defiant backlash of preservation. Efforts are now being made to halt the impending extinction of native languages, challenges are being leveled in court to broken treaties and land cessions, and American Indians everywhere seem fiercely determined to hold fast to their own traditions, and as St. Paul said in the Gospel, to hand down what they have received. It is not at all surprising that some of this renewed sense of cultural preservation has seeped into the Church, and in very many places there is a call for a new "Indian" way of being Catholic.

However, in some ways we seem to be heading farther away

from an authentic Indian Catholicism than ever. The liturgical innovations that followed in the wake of Vatican II have often, unfortunately, been implemented with little reference to what went before, and the new "Indian Masses" that began to be held up as models of Native worship were as dramatic a departure from the Indian Masses of old as the new "English Mass" was to Anglo-American Catholic practice of the 1950s.

Driving much of the new liturgical ethic, especially that of the Indian missions, was the concept of *inculturation*. It would be out of place to delve too deeply into the theoretical and anthropological aspects of inculturation in this book, but it has had a great influence on the changes of the last 40 years, and what has resulted is generally admitted by all parties, for good or ill, to be a dramatic break from the past.

In some cases, liturgical experimentalism has encouraged a hodge-podge of new practices with seemingly little discrimination as to history, tribal and regional culture, or even sacramental theology. Whatever the theoretical basis for such changes—and again, without judging the motives the participants—it looks to the more traditionally-minded as snipping disparate branches of American Indian culture and grafting them inartfully onto an already bare trunk of Latin Catholicism, shorn of most of the adornments which it had painstakingly grown over 1500 years.

It were as if, back in the waning days of the Roman Empire, a liturgical reformer had introduced mock gladiatorial combat at the Offertory, read the *Aeneid* and *Annales Maximi* from the pulpit, took the haruspicy at the altar of St. John Lateran, and made saints of Saturn, Aeneas, and Romulus. It takes no great historical acumen to realize that if such a thing had been proposed as the Roman Rite, it would not have lasted the century, much less to the present day.

For quite aside from the artfully crafted arguments of scholars and academics, the devout souls in the pews harbor their own opinions and tastes, and it must be frankly admitted that the most progressive liturgists have often been quite neglectful of the tastes of those who were devoted to the older liturgical forms.

xiii

Over the last 40 years, some of the more experimental attempts at inculturation have stirred up resentment among more traditionally-minded Catholics, both Indians and non-Indians alike. It was often Indians who first looked askance at what they themselves deemed "pagan rituals" being brought into the sanctuaries and who left the sacraments in frustration with the changes to the Mass. It is also true that a number of American Indians have come to appreciate certain aspects of the liturgical reform and of inculturation, viewing them as a vindication against those authorities within the Church who—at least within living memory—cooperated too often in a program of cultural destruction and assimilation. Such is the somewhat disjointed situation we have inherited.

I must admit at the outset that I cannot hope to comprehensively catalog all the relevant practices of the Indian missions. Time and travel constraints have allowed me only to sketch the barest outline of what could occupy many lifetimes of study by scholars better placed and trained than I. One can only do this subject justice by diligent study not only of the published sources but the copious manuscript archives at Kahnawake, Oka, Odanak and other missions as well as of the chancery archives of the bishops who oversaw them. Also crucially important would be to visit these locations and interview priests, choir members, and parishioners who still retain the living connections to some of the traditions described here. Finding myself unable to do all these things, I have been compelled to limit my scope to the *Jesuit Relations* and other primary sources, to liturgical handbooks for the laity primarily published in the 19th century, and to a few important manuscripts of which I have obtain copies. Supplementing these with some other sources I have collected over as yet only a few years of research, I am able only to touch on some of the key aspects of the traditional practices of the missions. There is little doubt that assumptions and conclusions that I have drawn from my limited sources will require substantial correcting in the years to come as more research is carried out.

Yet even a project of such limited scope has its place, if it be only to inspire researchers and liturgical historians to more deeply study the Indian Masses as a legitimate, organic development of the Roman Rite in North America. And then, please God, to use this knowledge to encourage future development that will be faithful to the Catholic traditions and sensibilities of the native peoples of the New World.

Claudio R. Salvucci, Mount Holly, NJ
April, 2008

+ Introduction +

All are present in the morning at the sacrifice of the Mass, which is celebrated in behalf of the whole village. Nearly all assist at the Mass of a second priest, and not a few at another if there be a third celebrant. While the first Mass of all, which is called "the Mission Mass," is being said, they sing sacred Hymns written in the vernacular tongue, and adapted to the feasts which are then being celebrated,—with a harmony truly beautiful, and not at all barbarous. Toward noon they assemble in the chapel for Vespers, which likewise consist in the singing of pious hymns. In these they use the cadence and the airs prescribed by Ecclesiastical law, and practiced in the churches of Europe.
—Letter from Fr. Louis Davaugour to Fr. Joseph Germain, 1710 (JR 66:151)

The liturgy first brought by the French to Canada and subsequently used at the missions was the classical Roman Rite as standardized after the Council of Trent. But as adaptations were made to the linguistic and cultural needs of the native Canadian peoples, minor divergences from Roman practice arose. The mission churches did not, of course, form any sort of *sui juris* Church independent of Roman canon law and patriarchal authority like the Maronite and other Eastern churches, nor can their liturgies even be satisfactorily compared with ancient Western rites like the Ambrosian or Mozarabic. But it is also clear that they showed a few distinct local variations from the Roman Missal that differentiated them from other Latin Rite areas in Europe and even in North America.

The first question that must be dealt with concerning these variations is whether they allow us to speak of a set of liturgical

1

"uses" in much the same way that we speak of the Sarum Use, a pre-Reformation liturgy from Salisbury in England, or the modern-day Anglican Use, a revised and corrected version of the *Book of Common Prayer* liturgy, currently used in the United States by some converts from the Episcopal church.

The case of the Indian Mass certainly differs from that of the Sarum and Anglican Uses—there is no question that both of the latter had different Missals and significant variations in the prayers the priests used at Mass. But it is very probable that the priest's portion of the Indian Mass did not differ to any great extent from the official Roman Missal. On this basis, it would seem hard to make the case for a separate use.

However, the Indian Masses did depart significantly from the Roman Missal in the parts sung by the schola, particularly the Propers. These sung texts—though they are all reduplicated by the priest—are not mere musical appendages to the priest's recitation but are liturgical in themselves, as is quite clearly expressed in the encyclical *Tra le Sollecitudini* of St. Pius X. The sung Propers are part of the liturgical books, are regulated by them, and are not capable of being emended or changed by the schola as, say, can easily be done with non-liturgical hymnody during Mass.

At the missions, the Roman Propers were not merely translated but were also rearranged and even replaced by newly composed Propers and prescribed hymns—with the result that even if the Indian Masses were back translated into Latin, they would still have shown significant divergences from the texts of the Roman Mass—enough divergences, in the opinion of the author, to warrant classifying them as new Uses in their own right.

A convenient name for this set of uses is not so easy to settle upon, and there does not seem to be any clear name given to us by history. The liturgy has been referred to as the "Mission Mass" and the "Indian Mass" (JR 66:151; Vecsey 1997:236). The latter term even has its equivalent in some native languages such as Micmac *lnu a'sutmamg* = "Native Mass" (see www.mikmaqonline.org), and is perhaps the most appropriate term for our purposes here.

It must be admitted though that these two designations in English may be rather too generic and also confusing outside of context. There are wholly different mission Masses elsewhere in the world, and the Indian Mass of Southeast Asia is a different thing entirely. Also, these terms only refer to the Mass and not to the other aspects that will be discussed here.

The Canadian Uses is one possible name, as almost all of the missions in question were located within (French) Canada, and the word Canada itself is taken from an Iroquois word meaning "town". The potential drawbacks are that this term seems to suggest a much larger territory than it actually encompasses, and also gives a false impression of it describing official uses of the modern Dominion of Canada. A more technically accurate designation, though it is unfortunately somewhat ungainly, would be the Algo-Iroquoian Uses, which has the benefit of focusing directly on the ethnic groups in question without confusing the issue with larger national or racial implications. Even more ungainly are, along the same lines as Syro-Malabar and Syro-Malankara, constructions like Romano-Algonquian and Romano-Iroquoian. These show the essentially Roman character of their ritual as opposed to, say, terms like Anglo-Algonquian and Anglo-Iroquoian for the various native versions of the Anglican *Book of Common Prayer* (see Appendix E). But those terms also compel us to break the obvious connection between the Algonquian missions and the Iroquoian missions, placing them into primarily linguistic groupings rather than liturgical ones.

None of these new coinages stand out as obviously ideal. So for the purposes of this book, tradition will be preferred and Indian Mass will be the term of choice employed for the liturgy of the missions as a whole. When we have need to refer to variations within a particular mission, the native name of the mission itself will suffice: the Kahnawake Use, the Oka Use, the Odanak Use, etc.

+ History +

In the earliest years of the colonial era, natives witnessed and participated in the Masses of the missionaries and of the French colonists. And it was probably not long before those missionaries gained an appreciation of the formidable linguistic barrier presented by an all-Latin liturgy among peoples that had not grown up with any familiarity with the language as an ecclesiastical or academic tongue.

So already in 1638, the *Pater Noster* and *Ave Maria* were being sung in Huron during Mass (JR 15:175). As is clear from a key quote from some years later in 1655, though the Hurons were singing texts in the vernacular, these were only sung as a devotional exercise during the liturgy in the manner of hymns and not as part of the liturgy itself:

> The Gloria in excelsis, the Credo, and the Pater are all sung in the Huron language, to the corresponding Church airs, by our innocent singers of both sexes; not that they chant the mass, but they sing during mass these hymns and holy prayers. (JR 41:151)

In time, however, these sung texts began to expand dramatically beyond the few common prayers taught to converts, and the Indians began to make increased use of the tremendous riches of Roman liturgical music. The impetus for this expansion seems to have been the establishment of dedicated Christian mission towns such as St. Francis Xavier du Sault (Kahnawake) and, apparently, a roughly contemporary indult or special permission from Rome authorizing the use of vernacular chant in the Masses of the Canadian missions.

This vernacular indult is assumed to exist but no such document has yet come to light. Fr. Yvan Forest stated flatly in 1951 that "of the origin of that privilege there is no trace anywhere. And nobody can state any date of the origin of it. Even the oldest priests used to refer to it as an 'immemorial tradition' of the old days." (Korolevsky 1957:183). Fr. Clement J. McNaspy made inquiries about it in the archives of Canada and Rome, but was unsuccessful in tracking it down (Higginson 1954).

So the evidence for the indult is presently only indirect. There is, first of all, the plain fact that mission books with vernacular chant were published with episcopal approval—which does not necessarily mean Roman approval but strongly suggests it. Moreover, there are historical sources that mention the indult. A translation from an 1878 preface to a Mohawk hymn book contains a particularly clear reference:

> Nevertheless the Church...has authorized, or at least tolerated in certain missions, above all among the savages*, the use of the chant in the native language during the services; the Holy See has even authorized this practice by an Indult accorded to the missions of the savages in the New World. It was after this Indult and the consent of our Lords the Bishops that this usage of the chant in the native tongue was conserved

---

* The word *savage* as found in many of the quotes here requires some explanation, as English speakers tend to read into it "mindless brute." But it is in most cases a translation of French *sauvage* which, in turn, came from the Latin *silvaticus*, meaning simply "forest dweller." In Canadian French, the word primarily has the sense of "undomesticated, wild" without necessarily implying brutish, mindless ferocity. As applied to the American natives, the French used *sauvage* rather neutrally the same way English speakers used *Indian*. And though many translators rendered it as *savage*, other English writers, perhaps sensing the semantic disparity between its usages in the two languages, have rendered it as *Indian*. A recent paper on the subject states flatly that *savage* in English gives "a misleading impression to English-speaking readers of how the early French missionaries and explorers regarded Canada's aboriginal people" (Franks 2002). In the interest of accuracy, the original wording of translations is retained in this book, and readers are asked to make the appropriate semantic adjustments on their own.

and preserved, particularly in the three villages of the Catholic faithful Iroquois in Canada. By means of this tolerance of the Church, the chant, for which these peoples have so much attraction and disposition, became like the complement to the sermon, the support of faith, the nourishment of piety among the savages. (ibid)

Assuming such an indult was granted, it probably came about in the late 1660s or early 1670s, when we begin to see the vernacular in contexts that is more properly liturgical. Fr. Pierre Cholenec (1641-1723) described the practice at the mission of St. Francis Xavier du Sault in 1677. In it, he mentions the use of the vernacular singing throughout the whole of the Mass—and particularly the *Credo*, which is placed exactly where it would liturgically be expected.

On Sunday morning the Father says Mass at 8 o'clock. The savages sing through nearly the whole of it, the men on one side and the women on the other, alternately and in 2 choirs. This they always do, at present, when they sing in the chapel,—in which also, for that purpose, the men are always placed on the Gospel side, and all the women on the other. After the Gospel, the Father preaches them a sermon, or has one preached to them by the Dogique, who is ever incomparable in this respect—as he again proved quite recently, on Christmas day...After the sermon, the Dogique intones the Credo in their language, in the Church plain-song, and they thus continue their chanting until the end of the Mass (JR 60:279-281)

Even more clear historical evidence of a move from devotional to liturgical singing is found in Fr. Claude Chauchetiere's report of 1679:

They formerly held Mass, or rather were merely present at Mass and at Vespers, which were sung by the French; but now they do everything themselves in their chapel ...This affection which the savages had for that chapel facilitated for them the means for learning the chants of the church — as, the hymns of the Blessed Sacrament, the hymns of the Virgin, and some others of the confessors and of the martyrs, the *inviolata*, the *veni creator*, the psalms, and more than thirty different hymns, alike for Mass and for Vespers and Benedictions. (JR 63:209–211)

Nonetheless, there still seems to have been something of a transitional period. While the repertoire of singing during Mass seems to have expanded dramatically to include some of the official liturgical prayers and hymns of the Church, some vestiges of the old practices of singing common devotional prayers apparently still remained.

A letter by the second bishop of Quebec in 1688 shows not only the specific texts that were being chanted and spoken at St. Francis Xavier at daily Mass but also some indication of how they were being affected by the liturgical year:

At the Introit of the Mass, the one among the men whom they call the Dogique, and who performs the office of Cantor, entones some hymn or some prose in their language, according to the diverse seasons of the year. In Easter time, O *filii*; around Pentecost, *Veni Creator*; in Advent, *Conditor alme siderum*; and the women unite their voices to those of the men creates a quite agreeable harmony. This chant is followed by the recitation of the Our Father, the Hail Mary, the Apostles' Creed, and certain acts which dispose them well to hear the holy Sacrifice. At the elevation is chanted the Hymn of the Blessed Sacrament and acts of adoration are made aloud. They finish by chanting the litanies of the Holy Virgin, and some people remain longer to say their chaplet. (Saint-Vallier 1856: 50; translation by the author)

In this description we see, first of all, "some hymn or some prose" serving as a seasonally variable Introit: and the three that are mentioned are taken right from the Roman Missal and Vespers: this is more in the realm of liturgical singing. But this chant is followed by the recitation of common prayers and "certain acts", which puts us back to devotional and not liturgical prayer. The chanting of the hymn of the Blessed Sacrament at the elevation could be seen a quasi-liturgical function, but with the acts of adoration and the litanies that follow, we are once again outside the sphere of liturgy.

Saint-Vallier the goes on to describe the Sunday Mass:

> On Sundays are added various things to the daily practices; one chants there a Mass of the Parish which begins with the blessed water, and from which no one dispenses himself, with the exception of the children for whom a low Mass is said afterward, which two among them serve in red robe and surplice. There is always an exhortation in the form of a preaching at the High Mass after the Gospel, and at the end is intoned the prayer for the King, which is observed also at the Mass of the children. (Saint-Vallier 1856:53)

The Mass of the Parish—i.e., the High Mass—is where the most significant development of the Indian Mass takes place, and where it reaches its full form.

In ensuing centuries, progressively more of the Roman texts began to be translated into various native languages and the Indian Masses began to assume more fixed forms, which were passed down from one missionary to another. Just as in the Middle Ages before the inventing of the printing press in Europe, priests in North America transmitted and stored their liturgical books in handwritten manuscripts. An elegantly written manuscript attributed to Jacques Bruyas and probably from ca. 1700, now in Lauinger Library at Georgetown University, already shows parts of the Mohawk liturgy. One page gives the native text for the *Asperges* under a simple illustration of the altar reminiscent of medieval illumination (Company 1996).

It was not until the mid-1800s that a number of the mission usages began to finally be published, as priests collated the earlier manuscript sources and compiled them into books for the laity called "paroissiens". A paroissien was a typically French phenomenon that was defined by Cabrol as "a kind of abridged Missal which includes the office of Benediction, several Litanies, morning and night prayers, etc. Vespers of Sunday (and sometimes Compline) are also included" (Cabrol 1934).

In the preface to his *Indian Good Book*, Eugene Vetromile touches on the interplay among the oral tradition of the Indians and the manuscript and published works which he drew from. He also gives his reasons for publication.

> The Tribes of the Abenakis...transmit the truths of the Catholic religion from parents to children, only by oral tradition. Rev. Edmund Demillier left a handwriting, containing a small prayer-book, which was a correction of the prayer-book printed by Rev. Mr. Romagné, with other additions. I have made use of them both, and I have spared no labor to correct them. But I found that this compilation was not sufficient to leave amongst the Indians a standing form of prayers and instructions in their own language. They needed a book to which they could have reference at this time, in which the spirit of infidelity, so widely prevailing among the white men, is endeavoring to find an access even to the red race. (Vetromile 1858a)

An extended description of the liturgies during this period, as seen in the paroissiens, is found in the next section.

Development of the Indian Masses continued through the first half of the 1900s, drawing inspiration from the liturgical movement that was then dawning throughout the Roman church. By 1927, Father Conrad Hauser, S.J. had adapted the liturgical books at St. Francis Xavier du Sault to the musical reforms of the early 20th century, and his work was carried on by other priests as well as by the members of the church's Indian choir. Twenty years later in 1947, Fr. Clement McNaspy attested to the continuance of liturgical development there:

> As this is being written, a new printed edition containing all the principal Gregorian masses, Credos, and frequently used hymns and canticles, is being bound for use here at Caughnawaga and at Saint-Régis...This new edition, with rhythm indicated according to the Solesmes theory, is the result of generations of study and adaptation of the Mohawk language rhythm to pre-existing Gregorian melodic patterns. It may well be the definitive edition. (McNaspy 1947)

Just a little over a decade away from the Second Vatican Council, McNaspy reported that Kahnawake's Mohawk-language liturgical library included almost all the Gregorian Masses as well as dozens of modern Mass settings, hundreds of polyphonic and modern motets, and Gregorian Propers for all Sundays, commons, and greater feasts: all the result, he said, "of years of painstaking adaptation." This description certainly leaves one with an appreciation of what the classical Indian Mass had become at its very height.

But it was not, unfortunately, to last. In 1969, the *Novus Ordo Missae* was promulgated by Pope Paul VI, and the traditional Roman Mass was completely reconfigured. In one sense, it was a vindication of the Indian Mass, as the Roman liturgy around the world had now adopted practices that previously were restricted to limited areas like the Indian missions—such as the use of the vernacular and in the substitution of hymns for Propers. Yet ironically, the Indian Masses themselves fell largely into disuse for the first time in 300 years of organic development.

Certainly, some aspects of the pre-conciliar liturgy still survived in the missions—particularly native-language hymnody. But a rather jarring discontinuity and loss of cultural patrimony was felt by some Indian Catholics for whom "Mass in the vernacular" meant something very different than what it meant to the Anglo-American Catholics around them:

> The Second Vatican Council changed the practice of Catholicism among the Indians at St. Regis. The Mohawks had been singing hymns in Mohawk for centuries, but their liturgy was otherwise strictly Latin rite. Vatican II encouraged the use of the vernacular at Mass, and in spite of all the emphasis on Iroquois nationalism of the 1960s, the first language on the reserve was now English. However, priests who introduced the English rite encountered resistance among older Mohawks who identified 'traditional Catholicism' with Mohawk and Latin. (Vecsey 1997: 112-113)

In some missions, Indian-language liturgies had apparently fallen into disuse before the Council. Teresa Sappier, the last survivng member of the Latin choir at St. Ann's at Old Town, does not remember Penobscot hymns being sung there—though she says that they would have been sung if their existence were known. Nonetheless, she personally remembered the Latin Masses with fondness and "tears in her eyes":

> It was true that the older people in the 1960s were very upset at the great loss of the Latin Mass. The ornate altar represented many holy things to our people and when it was ripped away, the Mass attendance attrition rate increased significantly. The priest was placed in the position where our beautiful Blessed Tabernacle once was and the Blessed Sacrament was placed off to the side. The Vatican II changes in the Church brought about deep sadness to many. Even today, I remember that shock, pain and sadness. (personal communication 2008)

As in the Latin Church at large, the abrupt and absolute manner in which the liturgy was reformed at the missions met with some pointed resistance. But the prevailing winds were largely against the defenders of tradition, and before long the old liturgy was practically, if not legally, defunct.

The notion of a distinctive Indian liturgy did not die, though its application shifted radically. In the years since the Council, it increasingly came to be associated with the kind of experimental inculturation carried out by the Tekakwitha Conference, the premier organization of Native Catholics in the world, founded by white priests in the 1939 but by this time becoming more and more run by native laymen.

One of the Conference's current stated goals is to "to deepen and affirm Native Catholic identity and pride in their culture and spiritual traditions", and to that end it has promoted some traditional practices such as native-language hymnody. But a good many new practices were imported into the Mass as well. A survey commissioned by the United States bishops at the turn of the millennium found the following symbols and rituals—some traditional, some new—being used as examples of American Indian inculturation in various dioceses throughout the country (USCCB 2002):

- Smudging (blessing, purifying) with cedar, sage, sweetgrass, and tobacco
- Eagle feather used in blessings
- Dance and drums used for liturgies
- Indian music in liturgy
- Indian naming ceremony in conjunction with Baptism
- Native attire used in local and diocesan celebrations
- Four-directional prayer
- Sweat lodge
- Statues, relics of Blessed Kateri Tekakwitha
- Medicine wheel
- Native crucifix and cross
- Sacred vessels, decorations, and vestments with Native designs

• Sacred pipe

Some of the more novel practices among these, despite some support within American Indian Catholic communities, became sources of contention not only with non-Indian Catholic traditionalists but also within Indian Catholic parishes themselves; some parishioners believing that such Indian customs, except for native-language hymns, did not belong in church (Vecsey 1997:120–121; 128).

And even forty years after the changes of the second Vatican Council, there still remains some attachment among liturgically conservative Indians to the old usages:

> Ojibway deacon Ron Boyer comments that in the first half of the twentieth century the old Indians had come to find meaning in the Latin mass.....Many of them did not want to lose the old mass with the Vatican II reforms. They resisted change, and even today some Anishinabe people speak of the Tridentine rite as the "Indian Mass" and ask permission to perform it on occasion. (Vecsey 1997:236)

The continued use of the term "Indian Mass" among the Ojibwe, Micmac and other tribes for the pre-Vatican II Mass is a rather striking irony, and one that has perhaps not been adequately appreciated. True, that it is an old term, and one sanctioned by custom—but it is still interesting that tribes are designating the old rite as a national liturgy rather than the new rite, which is supposed to be more culturally sensitive. Three centuries of tradition, it seems, still has something of a pull that has not been erased by subsequent innovation.

In the first decade of the new millenium, the liturgical landscape has shifted again in a grand and definitive way. Pope Benedict XVI's motu proprio *Summorum Pontificum*, in declaring that the Missal of 1962 was never abolished and affirming that it remains an integral part of the Latin Rite, has pointed the Roman Church toward a future where the modern and the traditional exist

A traditional Latin Mass—though not an Indian Mass—at St. Francis Xavier in Kahnawake. Photograph taken by the author, August 22, 2005.

side by side and with equal standing.

It remains to be seen what effect this new liturgical landscape will have on the mission usages. Among the youth of the missions, there is evidence of a traditionalist contingent, such as the two Potawatomi women in Kansas who "have joined an arch-conservative Catholic group at St. Mary's" and who wear veils and attend the Latin Mass—almost certainly the well-known Society of St. Pius X (SSPX) chapel there (Vecsey 1997:261). Whether this kind of traditionalism can translate into support for the Indian Mass is yet uncertain.

+ Sources +

A rather impressive collection of liturgical manuscripts still exists scattered throughout mission archives and secular libraries in the U.S. and Canada, and a number of these were edited and published during the mid-1800s and early 1900s. There is, therefore, an ample field for research, but as of yet it has gone largely unworked—although judging by the work of Paul André DuBois and others, the tide seems to be turning.

As it was not possible to review all of the relevant sources for this study, the descriptions here will focus on some the main ones: almost all published works from the middle to late 1800s. These books, to which extensive reference will be made in subsequent chapters, are described briefly below.

Book of Seven Nations

Fr. Jean André Cuoq's *Tsiatak Nihononwe*, or *Book of Seven Nations*, was published in 1865 for the mixed Iroquois and Algonquin mission of Oka, also known as Kanesatake. Most of the text is in Mohawk, with chant settings in that language for the ordinaries of Mass and other texts, and a section on songs for Mass and Vespers lists the Propers and hymns for all the Sundays of the liturgical year and the major feast days. A number of Mohawk prayers and devotions from Fr. Joseph Marcoux (1791–1855) at Kahnawake are then included, including the Stations of the Cross, the Rosary, and the novena to St. Francis Xavier. The final section is a supplement to canticles and prayers, and includes hymns in both Mohawk and Algonquin, prayers during Mass, the text of the Algonquin Mass, and some chants for the dismissal.

Kaiatonsera Teieriwakwatha

This work, published in 1890 for the Mohawk mission of St. Regis at Akwesasne and also apparently St. Francis Xavier du Sault at Kahnawake is one of the richest liturgical publications produced for the missions. The manuscript it is based on was written in 1878 and kept in the archives of the mission of St. Francis Xavier.

Almost entirely in Mohawk, the book features different settings of the ordinaries for Mass as well as sung Propers for Sundays, for important feast days throughout the year, and for the Common Masses of saints and other occasions. It also gives the texts for hymns and for Vespers. No author is listed on the title page, but the manuscript was written by Fr. Francis Xavier Marcoux (1805–1883), pastor at St. Regis from 1832 to his death, and Fr. Nicholas Victor Burtin (1828–1902), missionary at St. Francis Xavier from 1855 to 1892, serving as its pastor from 1864. The subtitle on the manuscript notes that Marcoux composed the chants for Mass and Vespers, and Pilling adds that Burtin, with the help of a member of the Indian choir, translated the vespers "into Caughnawaga" and set them to music.

Niina Aiamie Masinaigan

This book in Algonquin (really Nipissing, and not Cree as erroneously described in Pilling 1891) was compiled by the Oblate missionary Fr. Louis-Marie Lebret (1829–1903) from various different authors. It was published first in 1866 and then again in 1898 for the usage of the Indians of Temiscaming, Abitibi, Grand Lac, Lac Timagaming, Metadjiwang, and Weymontaching on the river St. Maurice. Many of the residents of these missions had emigrated in the 1850s from Lake of the Two Mountains (Oka/Kanasatake), so the texts in this book closely follow the Algonquin texts in the *Book of Seven Nations*.

This collection gives the Sunday Mass in Algonquin—including the Asperges, several Introits, and the servers' responses in Latin—

and it also gives the Requiem Mass and texts for Vespers, followed by hymn texts arranged by liturgical season and theme. There is no musical notation.

Collection of Huron Songs

A manuscript *Recueil de chants Hurons*, or *Collection of Huron songs*, now kept in the archives of the Séminaire du Quebec, dates from sometime before 1838. The manuscript was written by Paul Tsa8enhohi and contains the Mass in Huron along with a good number of hymns. It totals over 130 handwritten pages, but only the texts are given, without any music. Nonetheless, this work is particularly notable because it preserves the text of the "Huron Carol" attributed to St. Jean de Brébeuf, along with an accompanying translation in French.

The Maillard Manuscript

Abbé Pierre-Antoine-Simon Maillard (ca. 1710–1762) left a significant manuscript of about 360 pages of Micmac devotional, liturgical, and catechetical texts, compiled during the period 1757–1759. It contains prayers and all of the hours of the Divine Office in Micmac, ordinaries and Propers of the Mass, and hymns. The original is in the archives of the Séminaire du Quebec, a microfilmed copy of which is held by the American Philosophical Society in Philadelphia.

Paroissien Micmac

Fr. Pacifique de Valigny (1863–1943) in 1912 published a tiny but elegant volume *Alasotmamgeoel: Paroissien Micmac/Prayer-Book in Micmac*. It contains prayers; devotions such as the stations of the cross, rosary, and litanies; the forms for the Viaticum and Extreme Unction; the entire Divine Office from Matins to Compline;

the texts for High Mass, including the Asperges/Vidi Aquam, ordinaries, and Propers; and the text for Benediction of the Blessed Sacrament. This book was followed by the *Agantieoimgeoel Offices du Dimanche extrait du Paroissien Micmac* (1917), and the *Alasotmapegiatimgeoel, Paroissien Micmac singing book* (1923), the latter with 64 pages containing chant music for the Mass.

Indian Good Book

This work was compiled by Fr. Eugene Vetromile (1819-1881) and published in several editions (1856, 1857, and a considerably expanded edition of 1858). Vetromile draws from a number of manuscripts in several different languages, and the 1858 edition has Masses in Penobscot, Micmac, and Montagnais. It includes the Propers of the Requiem in Penobscot and Micmac as well as the Micmac Propers for the festival of the Blessed Virgin Mary and for Christmas day. Vespers are given in Latin, Penobscot, and Micmac; and there is also Compline in Micmac and the Little Office of the Blessed Virgin in Latin and Penobscot. A few of the sacramental formulas are given as well—including the Baptismal interrogations in Penobscot and Passamaquoddy; the Baptismal formula itself in Passamaquoddy, Penobscot, Micmac, and Montagnais; and the formula of marriage in Penobscot and Passamaquoddy.

The *Indian Good Book* does not contain any actual music, but some Penobscot chant is featured in a smaller work by Vetromile, *Ahiamihewintuhangan; The Prayer Song* (1858), which includes Mass ordinaries for Christmas night and some litanies and hymns for other liturgical occasions.

Aiamie Kushkushkutu Mishinaigan

This small book was printed for the Montagnais missions of the Saguenay and Tadoussac, and is ascribed to Fr. Flavien Durocher (1800-1876), who arrived at Saguenay in 1844 and published this

The cover of Fr. Pacifique's *Alasotmamgeoel*, or *Paroissien Micmac* (1912).

work three years later. It gives the text and chant notation for two Masses, a Requiem Mass, and Vespers, along with some other material.

Other Sources

Rounding out the actual liturgical sources are a few historical ones which touch upon the practices of the missions—many of which we have had occasion to mention already.

Unquestionably the most useful collection of primary source material is the *Jesuit Relations* (here abbreviated JR), which covers almost two centuries of missionary activity from 1610 to 1791 over the entire area of New France. The original texts alongside a particularly accessible English translation were published from 1896 to 1901 under the direction of Reuben Gold Thwaites. This collection contains copious material on the liturgical and devotional life of the missions, particularly for the 1600s.

The *Estat présent de l'Église et de la colonie française dans la Nouvelle-France* (1688) of Jean-Baptiste de Saint-Vallier (1653–1727), the second bishop of Quebec, contains particularly good information for St. Francis Xavier du Sault in its infancy. The *Histoire des Abenakis* (1866) by Abbé J. A. Maurault (1819–1871) provides a number of interesting Christian customs of that tribe.

+ The Liturgy of the Indian Mass +

Though liturgical practices varied from mission to mission, there are enough commonalities overall to allow us to discuss the Indian Masses as a group of closely related uses. It should be understood that the following discussion pertains to the standard sung High Mass of Sundays and important feast days.

The priest's portion of the Mass and the congregation's responses all remained in Latin, as indicated quite clearly in a number of the mission liturgical books (*Book of Seven Nations*, p. 419-421; *Niina Aiamie Masinaigan*, 40-42). The one exception may be the Micmac mission at Restigouche; in the *Micmac Paroissien* and elsewhere, the responses for the Asperges, the introduction to the Gospel, the introduction to the Preface, and the Communion are given in both Latin and Micmac—though it is possible that the Micmac here was simply listed for translation purposes and may not actually have been sung by the congregation.

In all of the missions, however, those parts of the Mass sung by the schola or choir—the ordinaries and Propers—were generally in the vernacular. Such extensive use of the vernacular may not seem striking today, but prior to the 1960s, to sing Propers or ordinaries in the vernacular was strictly forbidden throughout most of the Latin Church and was the select privilege of only a very few places.

The ordinaries at the missions were for the most part simply translated wholesale into the target languages. The only major exceptions were in the missions of the Algonquins and the Montagnais, among whom the Kyrie was in Greek. Also anomalous are some Micmac liturgies, which give the Kyrie in the vernacular but in a troped form with additional phrases added into the liturgical text—a practice that was common in the High Middle Ages but fell out of favor again after the Council of Trent. The

Depictions of various portions of the Indian Mass, from Vetromile's *Indian Good Book* (1858).

Micmac Kyrie shows a standard form in the *Indian Good Book*, but the Paroissien Micmac and athe Maillard manuscript give troped versions of the Kyrie and Agnus Dei.

However, the sung Propers at the missions followed a rather different system than they did in the Roman Missal. They generally consisted of an Introit, a Gradual and/or Alleluia/Tract or sometimes simply a hymn, an Offertory hymn, and a Communion hymn. Thus, especially among the Mohawk, vernacular hymns took the place of many of the sung Roman Propers, particularly the Offertory and the Communion verses. It is quite probable that the priest recited the Latin Propers on his own *sotto voce*, but at any rate there is no indication that the schola sung these.

Among all the mission Propers, the Introits are undoubtedly the most interesting. While all the Masses show true Introits, the number of them was often dramatically reduced, and they did not follow the pattern laid out in the Roman Missal. Introits were often reused over whole liturgical seasons, with a small number rotating duty throughout the entire year.

For example, in the *Book of the Seven Nations*, the Introit for the whole season of Advent is the *Terribilis est*, which in the Roman Missal is used only for the dedication of a Church. During Christmastide and through the Sundays after Epiphany is used the *Aete8atsennonni*, apparently a variation of the Roman *Gaudeamus*. Septuagesima sees the *Terribilis* again, whose use continues throughout Lent until Passion Sunday, when the *Sirisare* is used. Eastertide returns to the *Aete8atennonni*, though with some change in wording. The *Karo kase*, the Iroquois version of the Veni Creator, comes in at Pentecost, followed immediately by the *Terribilis* at Trinity Sunday and, apparently, for all of the Sundays after Pentecost. The Introits for a few fixed-day feasts are as follows: *At8atsennonni* for the Assumption, *Tek8aoron8anions* for the Immaculate Conception, and *Sirisare* for the Precious Blood.

The Introits in the *Niina Aiamie Masinaigan* for the Algonquin missions are not listed under particular Sundays or seasons, but the cycle of them seems to have been very similar, if not the same, as their parent mission of Oka. Five Introit texts are listed between the *Asperges* and the *Kyrie* of the Algonquin Mass: the *Gaudeamus*, *Terribilis*, *Reminiscere*, *Mino Manito Okijikom* and *Salve Sancta Parens*. Two of these also appear in the *Book of Seven Nations*: the *Terribilis* and the *Gaudeamus*.

The *Collection of Huron Songs* gives only the *Salve Sancta Parens*. The *Aiamie Kushkushkutu Mishinaigan* from the Montagnais missions contains two Introits: the first is the *Terribilis*, a point of similarity with the Algonquin missions of Oka and the north. The second, interestingly, is the beginning of the *Our Father*—perhaps a vestige of the early days when common prayers were sung during Mass. A Montagnais Mass in Vetromile's *Indian Good Book* also begins with the *Our Father* as an Introit, and a note there tells us that this Mass was written by a Fr. La Brosse. Two Introits are given for the Penobscot Mass in the *Indian Good Book*: one for Sunday Mass and one for the feasts of the Blessed Virgin.

The Micmac Introits at Restigouche were somewhat unique, as they were apparently freshly composed from seasonally appropriate passages from the Vulgate. As given in the Maillard manuscript, the Introit for the Sundays in Advent is *Haec dicit Dominus exercituum* from Haggai 2:7, that of Christmas day is *Evangelizo vobis gaudium magnum* from Luke 2:10-12; and for all of Lent *Vivo ego, dicit Dominus* from Ezekiel. Another unsourced Introit is listed in the same place as the ordinaries; perhaps this one was used during the rest of the year. The Micmac Masses also show Graduals and Alleluias as well as Offertory verses and, interestingly, verses that are called in the Maillard manuscript and in the *Indian Good Book* "post-communion" though in the *Micmac Paroissien* they are labeled "communion".

The Mohawk *Kaiatonsera Teieriwakwatha* shows us a greatly expanded system of Propers than anything seen in the other books. There is a very full set of Masses here for the liturgical year, including even the common Masses for saints and votive Masses, and most of the Sundays and major feasts throughout the year have their own Introits. There are only a few repetitions, mainly within the same liturgical season, and there are also unique Introits for the common

26

IOTIIATATOKENTI IAHTE IOTINAKWA-IENTERHAON.

Iontaw.
T 5.

Sewenni-io, io- nehrakwat tsini sheten - rrn io-

iata - to-ken - ti nonwa ken weute karonhiake she - te-

run, iahte ka - kont on-tsen-non - ni. (*sh.*) A - re-

ri - ia a- re - ri- ia. Iakotaskat iaht · iakoiatorohon ie kari-

wa- nerea, ne iakotahitakhe Rawenniio raoiane-ren-se-rake.
Ahon... *Takw.* (*sk.* 63). *Katke onte* (*sk.* 141).

T 8.

A - re - ri - ia, are - ri - ia. Tsi-ni

kaia-ti - - io nok io - kwatse sa- tonnhe - - tston,

ionehrakwat tsi - ni hianonwehon Rawenni - io.
Swanikonhrarak (*sk.* 137). *Tetewariwak tsini* (*sk.* 181)

IOKARENRE

T 1.

Ne io - ia- ta - to-ken- ti wat-tokhakwe iahte io- na-

kwaienter- ha-on. (*sh.*) A - re-ri - ia. *Satkon Nib.* l i.

Common of Virgins of the Akwesasne Use, from the *Kaiatonsera Teieriwakwatha* (p. 257). At the top of the page is the chant for the Introit *Sewenniio*. Below that are notations in italics that refer to the appropriate melody for the Kyrie *Takw[entenr Anen]* and other ordinaries on page 63 as well as to the text of the hymn *Katke onte* on page 141, here taking the place of the Gradual. The chant for the *Areriia* or Alleluia follows, then a reference to two more hymns: *Swanikonhrarak* on page 137, and *Tetewariwak tsini* on page 181, which almost certainly were sung as the Offertory and at Communion respectively. The bottom of the page shows the very beginning of Vespers, *Iokarenre*. This particular Mass could appropriately be used for the modern feast of Blessed Kateri Tekakwitha, although of course her feast had not yet been instituted when this book was published. The chant melodies of the Introit and Alleluia were adapted from the first Mass of a Virgin Martyr *Loquebar* of the Roman *Liber Usualis*.

of saints. All told, the *Kaiatonsera* gives about 40 different Introits. Graduals do not appear, but each feast and Sunday includes an Alleluia verse. The Offertory and Communion verses are absent, and references to two or more hymns are given instead.

The Indian Masses all have versions of the five Roman Sequences that were used in the post-Tridentine period: the *Victimae Paschali Laudes* for Easter, *Veni Sancte Spiritus* for Pentecost, *Lauda Sion Salvatorem* for Corpus Christi, *Dies Irae* for the Requiem Mass, and the *Stabat Mater* for Our Lady of Sorrows.

But there are also some additional Sequences in the missions uses as well. *Sacrae Familiae* was traditionally sung in the diocese of Quebec for the original feast of the Holy Family instituted by Bishop Laval for the third Sunday of Easter. Fr. Charles-Amador Martin (1648–1711) has been credited with composing the chant of the Mass and office for the feast, though perhaps he was only responsible for the Sequence itself (Langevin 1874:266). The Mohawk version, *Iesos Wari Sose*, is given for the feast of the Holy Family both in the *Book of Seven Nations* and the *Kaiatonsera Teieriwakwatha*, and an Algonquin version, *Jezos, Mani, Josep*, is found in the *Niina Aiamie Masinaigan*. The *Kaiatonsera Teieriwakwatha* gives other Sequences: *Tehnironhiakehronon* for Trinity Sunday and *Hetsitwasennaien nonwa* for the feast of St. Francis Xavier at Kahnawake as well as (with slight modifications) the feast of St. Regis at Akwesasne, the respective patronal saints of each mission.

It is not evident from the sources whether the Epistle and Gospel were read in the vernacular only. The *Book of Seven Nations* gives the Sunday Gospel readings in Mohawk, but it is possible that the practice was, as occurs with the Missal of 1962 in English-speaking Catholic parishes today, for the priest to give the readings in Latin and to then re-read them again in the vernacular at the homily.

The table on the following page shows the structure of a generalized Algonquian-Iroquoian High Mass.

Schola or Choir in the Vernacular	Priest / Deacon in Latin
Asperges/Vidi Aquam (on Sunday)	
Introit	Prayers at the Foot of the Altar
Kyrie	Kyrie (silently) ?
Gloria	Gloria (silently) ?
	Collect
	Epistle
Hymn or Gradual	Gradual (silently) ?
Sequence (if any)	
	Gospel
	Homily
Creed	Creed (silently) ?
Offertory Hymn	Offertory Verse ?
	Secret (silently)
	Preface
Sanctus	Sanctus (silently) ?
	Canon (silently)
	Pater Noster
Agnus Dei	Agnus Dei (silently) ?
Communion Hymn	Communion Verse (silently) ?
	Postcommunion
	Dismissal
	Last Gospel

To show what the full Mass would have been in practice, I have included an entire Mass from the Use of Akwesasne in Appendix A, along with some of the ordinaries from other missions.

Requiem Mass

The Requiem Mass is given very special attention in all of the mission publications, and it deserves a separate treatment. In the Mohawk missions, the Mass of the Dead adhered very scrupulously to the Roman Propers and their established chants. The *Book of Seven Nations* gives Mohawk versions of the proper Introit *Requiem Aeternam*, Gradual *Requiem Aeternam*, Tract *Absolve*, Sequence *Dies Irae*, Offertory *Domine Jesu*, and Communion *Lux Aeterna* for the Kanesatake Use. In the section for the feast of All Souls, the Requiem according to the Kahnawake Use is also listed: here all the Propers are given, and a motet is added between the Offertory and Communion verses. The Use of Akwesasne is given in the *Kaiatonsera Teieriwakwatha*, where again, all the Propers are found.

The Algonquian-speaking missions, however, omitted some of the Propers. The Algonquin Masses in the *Book of Seven Nations* and in the *Niina Aiamie Masinaigan* only give an Introit and the *Dies Irae*—the Gradual, Tract, Offertory, and Communion do not appear. The same arrangement is found in the Montagnais Mass in the *Aiamie Kushkushkutu Mishinaigan*.

The Penobscot Requiem in the *Indian Good Book* gives an Introit, the *Dies Irae*, and an Offertory, omitting the Gradual, Tract, and Communion verse but also adding a text in Latin for the holy souls, *O salutaris hostia sacra*, probably sung at the elevation. The Micmac Requiem in this book has the Introit, *Dies Irae*, Offertory, and Communion, and is thus fairly complete save for the Gradual and Tract. It also gives a text for the elevation.

Therefore, for many of the missions, the Requiem Masses show the same pattern as the regular Masses—all of them show an Introit and the *Dies Irae* Sequence, but many of the other Propers are omitted. Only the Mohawk uses retain the full set of Propers (see table on the following page).

Requiem Mass	Introit: Requiem Aeternam	Gradual: Requiem Aeternam	Tract: Absolve	Sequence: Dies Irae	Offertory: Domine Jesu	Communion: Lux Aeterna	other
Book of Seven Nations (Kanesatake)	√	√	√	√	√	√	* Pie Jesu post-Sanctus. Burial: Libera, etc.
Book of Seven Nations (Kahnawake)	√	√	√	√	√	√	* Motet between offertory and communion
Kaiatonsera Teieriwakwatha	√	√	√	√	√	√	* Libera, etc.
Book of Seven Nations (Algonquin)	√			√			* Libera, etc.
Niina Aiamie Masinaigan	√			√			* Libera, etc.
Indian Good Book (Penobscot)	√			√	√		* O Salutaris hostia sacra, between Sanctus and Agnus Dei. Libera, etc.
Indian Good Book (Micmac)	√			√	√	√	* Hymn? For at the elevation; Libera, etc.
Aiamie Kushkushkutu Mishinaigan	√			√			Libera

Vernacular propers of the Requiem Mass as given in the various mission books. The Mohawk uses follow the Roman liturgy most closely in giving all the correct propers. The Gradual, Tract, and sometimes the Offertory and Communion are typically omitted in the Algonquian-speaking missions.

Other Liturgical Customs

Two special rituals within the Mass should also be mentioned: those of the pax board and the *pain benit*.

The pax board, also called the pax-brede or osculatorium, was a custom that arose in Europe in the Middle Ages to exchange the sign of peace at Mass by means of a tablet that depicted some holy scene, particularly the crucifixion. This tablet was kissed first by the priest, who then passed it on to the acolytes, after which it was offered to the laity at the Communion rail.

At St. Francis Xavier du Sault in 1947, the rite of the pax board had survived in a somewhat different liturgical context at the offertory, for the feast of St. John the Baptist and for Easter:

> Preserved in the same fire-proof vault with Kateri's relics are several rare liturgical treasures. One of the more exceptional is an "instrument of peace"; it looks very much like an illuminated scroll, with figures of Christ, Mary and St. John in high relief. Here in Caughnawaga it is not used at the "pax" of the High Mass, but is exposed to public veneration on specified occasions. Every year, for instance, on the feast of St. John the Baptist (patronal feast of Quebec and celebrated both religiously and otherwise as a national holiday) the age-old St. John the Baptist Temperance Society offers Mass in a body. At the offertory the priest descends to the altar rail with the "instrument of peace" for each member to kiss, a pledge of fidelity to Christ in this important matter of temperance. On Easter Sunday this year, I was privileged to pass the "instrument of peace" at the Offertory (McNaspy 1947).

Another old liturgical survival at Kahnawake is the *panis benedictus* or *pain benit*, bread that was brought to Mass and given a special blessing, after which it was distributed to the congregation and then was eaten in the Church or taken home. This custom had prevailed chiefly in France and, by extension, in Quebec, but the

1917 *Catholic Encyclopedia* already stated that it had "almost entirely disappeared" by that date.

Nonetheless, its survival and importance at St. Francis Xavier du Sault in the 1940s was attested by McNaspy in describing a Mass he attended on Easter Sunday:

> Just after the Vidi Aquam we performed another ancient liturgical rite almost unknown in North America save for Caughnawaga: the blessing of the bread. Hundreds of specially prepared loaves (contributed this year by the Holy Name Society) were arranged in baskets and in a high steeple-like form, twenty feet high, festooned with varied flags and crowned by British and American banners....The bread is blessed according to one of the several forms given in the Roman Ritual, then distributed during Mass to the entire congregation. Caughnawagans are visibly appreciative of the "panis benedictus," and during centuries of its use here have attributed semi-miraculous effects to this sacramental. When you observe their attitude you realize that here is a living tradition, no mere archaeological survival (ibid).

The Abenaki also shared this Easter Sunday tradition. J. A. Maurault reported in 1866 that they carefully kept their blessed bread received that day for a whole year, and some still maintained pious superstitions that it protected them against accidents, helped them in hunting, and had extraordinary medicinal virtues as well (Maurault 1866:570–571).

Liturgical Languages

> *I remain convinced that the day when the Iroquois will have lost their maternal language, they will at the same time be definitively lost for the faith.*
> —Bishop Joseph Alfred Langlois of Valleyfield, Quebec, 1934 (Vecsey 1997:111)

Theoretically any rite of the Church can be rendered into in any language, so language is not used to demarcate one liturgical rite or use from another. The use of these vernacular in the Algonquian and Iroquoian missions made these somewhat unusual in the Catholic world, though other areas such as China and Croatia were also permitted to have portions of the Mass in the vernacular.

As it pertains to the Indian missions, the term "vernacular" needs to be qualified to a certain extent. Although generally, the language used at each mission was the language of the major ethnic group that inhabited it, certain idioms tended to become standardized languages of prayer which were often different languages than were natively spoken.

This was especially the case in the 1600s with Huron. Refugees and captives from the Huron missions were the first to bring Christianity into Iroquoia, and their language became the preferred one for prayer. Fr. François le Mercier reported in 1655 that Iroquois women at Quebec were learning Christian songs in the Huron language (JR 41:221). Huron continued in use after the foundation of the Iroquois mission of St. Francis Xavier du Sault (JR 63:149), and Fr. Luc-François Nau (1703–1753) was still attesting to its prevalance as late as 1735:

> Iroquois and Huron are the only two difficult languages; we must, however, be familiar with them both in our mission, because all the prayers are in Huron....All our savages understand Huron, and prefer it to Iroquois, although the pronunciation is not so pleasing to the ear. Hence it is that they do not care to recite their

prayers in their own native tongue. (JR 68:279)

Nonetheless, Mohawk eventually ousted Huron as the language of prayer at the Iroquois missions: Huron is absent, for example, from the *Book of Seven Nations* and the *Kaiatonsera Teiriwakwatha*.

By the 19th century, the liturgical idiom of the mixed Algonquin and Nipissing population at Oka became fixed as the Nipissing dialect, even though the missionaries called it, confusingly, "Algonquin". This mission was also an interesting case as it was also home to a sizable community of Iroquois, and both languages were used at the mission: the *Book of Seven Nations* gives separate Mohawk and Algonquin Masses, but hymns in Algonquin are also scattered among the Iroquois Propers for the year; something that we do not find, for instance, at Kahnawake or Akwesasne.

In the missions of the Algonquians we find a little more diversity—the *Indian Good Book* contains Masses in Micmac and Abenaki, and Vetromile mentions in it that some Passamaquoddy used the Kennebec language for some of their devotions and that they generally knew the Catechism in Penobscot (Vetromile 1858a: 268, 299). Verwyst relates in his biography of Baraga regarding the Menominee that "on Sundays the Indians used to sing during holy Mass the pious hymns they had learned in Chippewa. At first F. Skolla preached to them in Chippewa, and although their knowledge of that language was somewhat imperfect, they listened to him with great attention." He also mentions the Indians of Arbre Croche singing hymns in Ottawa during Mass (Verwyst 1900: 49, 405).

Also, it is important to note that different styles existed even within the same language. St. Jean de Brébeuf describes a style of speech known in Huron as *acwentonch*, which was used by all the nearby Indians during councils and was a special style of raising and quavering the voice like that of a Preacher. He states explicitly that it was unlike the common speech (JR 10:257). The use of a special ceremonial style within Native American languages is very common:

> Prayer may be a universal category, but there is considerable cross-cultural variation about what constitutes a prayer and the role it plays in the culture. It is often in a special ceremonial style, set apart from other types of ceremonial speech. It is always highly structured, and sometimes a set, memorized speech. Special paralinguistic features are common. For example, the Delaware and Shawnee use a special sentence intonation, a flat monotone with a sharp drop at the end (Ives Goddard, personal communication 1975). (Wick R. Miller 1996)

Miller further notes that ceremonial speech is very common and that it is well developed among those cultures who prize ceremonialism—even to the extent of being regarded as sacred. To what extent the composition and recitation of Christian prayers drew upon these existing ceremonial styles and were set apart from the common speech would be an interesting avenue for linguistic research.

+ Calendar and Hagiography +

In general, the missions do not show very great deviations in the calendar, except that in the Canadian missions, the feast of the Holy Family was formerly celebrated on the 3rd Sunday of Easter, following the former usage of Quebec. Now it is generally celebrated in the *Novus Ordo Missae* on the Sunday after Christmas and, in the 1962 missal, on the Sunday in the octave of the Epiphany.

A complete daily liturgical calendar is preserved in the *Book of Seven Nations* and it shows—expectedly—a number of peculiarly French saints (see Appendix C).

The *Kaiatonsera Teieriwakwatha* does not give a full liturgical calendar, but two definite peculiarities are notable in its Masses for Sundays and the principal feasts. First, the Mohawk names for three of the seasons anticipate the subsequent feast, unlike in the Roman Missal where they refer back to the previous one:

Roman Missal		Kaiatonsera Teieriwakwatha
Sundays after Epiphany	=	Sundays until Septuagesima
Sundays after Easter	=	Sundays until Ascension
Sundays after Pentecost	=	Sundays until Advent

The second peculiarity is in the arrangement of Masses for these seasons. For the Sundays until Septuagesima (i.e., after Epiphany), there are three Masses listed by number not by name (I, II, III). Similarly, for the Sundays until Advent (i.e., after Pentecost) there are four Masses listed again by number (I, II, III, IV). There is no apparent indication whether these Masses were used *ad libitum* or rotated within these seasons according to some fixed rule. Only one Mass is listed for the Sundays until Ascension (i.e., after

37

Tsinahe thonakeraton Iesos.	Niiohne.	7 Niwa- sontashen.	Tsi naontata- tkenroserawe.	Tsi nonsa- hatonnhete.	Karonhiake sonsarete.	Niio rawentawen.	Awentokon.	Ion tsi ra- thonniane.
1891	d	25 Jan.	11 Febr.	29 Mar.	7 Mai.	28 Mai.	27	29 Nov.
1892	c b	14 Febr.	2 Mar.	17 Apr.	26 Mai.	16 Jun.	24	27 Nov.
1893	A	29 Jan.	15 Febr.	2 Apr.	11 Mai.	1 Jun.	27	3 Dec.
1894	g	21 Jan.	7 Febr.	25 Mar.	3 Mai.	24 Mai.	28	2 Dec.
1895	f	10 Febr.	27 Febr.	14 Apr.	23 Mai.	13 Jun.	25	1 Dec.
1896		2 Febr.	19 Febr.	5 Apr.	14 Mai.	4 Jun.	26	29 Nov.
1897	c	14 Febr.	3 Mar.	18 Apr.	27 Mai.	17 Jun.	24	28 Nov.
1898	b	6 Febr.	23 Febr.	10 Apr.	19 Mai.	9 Jun.	25	27 Nov.
1899	A	29 Jan.	15 Febr.	2 Apr.	11 Mai.	1 Jun.	27	3 Dec.
1900	g	11 Febr.	28 Febr.	15 Apr.	24 Mai.	14 Jun.	25	2 Dec.
1901	f	3 Febr.	20 Febr.	7 Apr.	16 Mai.	6 Jun.	26	1 Dec.
1902	e	26 Jan.	12 Febr.	30 Mar.	8 Mai.	29 Mai.	27	30 Nov.
1903	d	8 Febr.	25 Febr.	12 Apr.	21 Mai.	11 Jun.	25	29 Nov.
1904	c b	31 Jan.	17 Febr.	3 Apr.	12 Mai.	2 Jun.	26	27 Nov.
1905	A	19 Febr.	8 Mar.	23 Apr.	1 Jun.	22 Jun.	24	3 Dec.
1906	g	11 Febr.	28 Febr.	15 Apr.	24 Mai.	14 Jun.	25	2 Dec.
1907	f	27 Jan.	13 Febr.	31 Mar.	9 Mai.	30 Mai.	27	1 Dec.
1908	e d	16 Febr.	4 Mar.	19 Apr.	28 Mai.	18 Jun.	24	29 Nov.
1909	c	7 Febr.	24 Febr.	11 Apr.	20 Mai.	10 Jun.	25	28 Nov.
1910	b	23 Jan.	9 Febr.	27 Mar.	5 Mai.	26 Mai.	27	27 Nov.
1911	A	12 Febr.	1 Mar.	16 Apr.	25 Mai.	15 Jun.	25	3 Dec.
1912	g f	4 Febr.	21 Febr.	7 Apr.	16 Mai.	6 Jun.	26	1 Dec.
1913	e	19 Jan.	5 Febr.	23 Mar.	1 Mai.	22 Mai.	28	30 Nov.
1914	d	8 Febr.	25 Febr.	12 Apr.	21 Mai.	11 Jun.	27	29 Nov.
1915	c	31 Jan.	17 Febr.	4 Apr.	13 Mai.	3 Jun.	26	28 Nov.
1916	b A	20 Febr.	8 Mar.	23 Apr.	1 Jun.	22 Jun.	24	3 Dec.
1917	g	4 Febr.	21 Febr.	8 Apr.	17 Mai.	7 Jun.	26	2 Dec.
1918	f	27 Jan.	13 Febr.	31 Mar.	9 Mai.	30 Mai.	27	1 Dec.
1919	e	16 Febr.	5 Mar.	20 Apr.	29 Mai.	19 Jun.	24	30 Nov.
1920	d c	1 Febr.	18 Febr.	4 Apr.	13 Mai.	3 Jun.	26	28 Nov.
1921	b	23 Jan.	9 Febr.	27 Mar.	5 Mai.	26 Mai.	27	27 Nov.
1922	A	12 Febr.	1 Mar.	16 Apr.	25 Mai.	15 Jun.	25	3 Dec.
1923	g	28 Jan.	14 Febr.	1 Apr.	10 Mai.	31 Mai.	27	2 Dec.
1924	f e	17 Febr.	5 Mar.	20 Apr.	29 Mai.	19 Jun.	24	30 Nov.
1925	d	8 Febr.	25 Febr.	12 Apr.	21 Mai.	11 Jun.	25	29 Nov.
1926	c	31 Jan.	17 Febr.	4 Apr.	13 Mai.	3 Jun.	26	28 Nov.
1927	b	13 Febr.	2 Mar.	17 Apr.	26 Mai.	16 Jun.	24	27 Nov.
1928	A g	5 Febr.	22 Febr	8 Apr.	17 Mai.	7 Jun.	26	2 Dec.
1929	f	27 Jan.	13 Febr.	31 Mar.	9 Mai.	30 Mai.	27	1 Dec.
1930	e	16 Febr.	5 Mar.	20 Apr.	29 Mai.	19 Jun.	24	30 Nov.

Major feasts for 1891–1930 from the *Kaiatonsera Teieriwakwatha* (1890), with the dates for Septuagesima Sunday, Ash Wednesday, Easter, Ascension, Corpus Christi, and the first Sunday of Advent. The next-to-last column (*Awentokon*) gives the number of Sundays after Pentecost.

Easter), but this single Mass has a total of 12 hymns for Offertory and Communion. Undoubtedly these hymns would have varied each Sunday while the Introit and Alleluia remained the same. Interestingly, however, all of the Sundays within these seasons have their own unique Vespers—so it is only the Mass Propers that repeat themselves.

One unusual example of a native Christian calendar—though it is not liturgical—is the Cree calendar of Albert Lacombe for 1882 (see the following page). On the left are listed the months in French with the devotions particular to them. On the right are listed the native months in Cree syllabics with visual depictions corresponding to the month names. In the center is the calendar for the year, with Sundays marked as Xs and weekdays as straight lines.

The feast of the universally acclaimed patron saint of the Indian missions, Kateri Tekakwitha, was not instituted until 1980 with her beatification, and invoking her formally in the liturgy prior to this time would have been forbidden. Yet every year on April 17th, Indian and French Catholics celebrated a votive Mass of the Holy Trinity at Kahnawake in her memory—thus commemorating the date of her death but not violating the prohibition of a public *cultus*:

> Every year on the anniversary of the death of Good Catharine—la Bonne Catherine, (this being the name under which, out of respect for the Holy See, this holy virgin is honored in Canada) several parishes in the neighborhood come to chant in the Church of Sault St. Louis a solemn Mass of the Holy Trinity. A parish priest at Lachine, a town on Montreal Island, by name Mr. Remy, who recently arrived from France, on being informed by his parishioners of this custom, replied that he deemed it a duty not to sanction by his presence a public cultus not yet permitted by the Church. Most, on hearing him speak thus, could not refrain from

The Cree Calendar for 1882 by Albert Lacombe (as reproduced in Pilling 1891:284a). The month names and the devotions proper to them are given on the left in French. The native month names are on the right in Cree syllabics, with corresponding visual depictions. Sundays are marked with X, weekdays with I, feast days with superscript [x], days of fast and abstinence with superscript [o]. The underline from late February to early April marks the Lenten season.

saying that he would soon be punished for his refusal, and in fact he fell dangerously ill the same day. He at once understood the cause of this unexpected attack. He bound himself by a vow to follow the example of his predecessors, and was instantly cured. (Charlevoix 1900, vol. 4:296)

The extant mission books do not give a great deal of attention to the eight Canadian or North American martyrs, including St. Jean de Brébeuf and St. Isaac Jogues. They were only beatified in 1925 and canonized in 1930, so like Kateri their *cultus* also would have been prohibited prior to this time. But an 1885 letter from the residents of Kahnawake to Rome, petitioning mainly for the canonization of Blessed Kateri, did not fail to mention two of the martyrs as well:

There are two others who though Frenchmen are still for us as if they were our own, because they taught our ancestors the Sign of the Cross and the way of salvation, and were therefore put to death by the wicked. These two also we should like to hold in veneration as our protectors, our advocates. Their names are Father Isaac Jogues and Brother René Goupil. (*Positio*:448)

In more recent times, quite contrary to the warm language of this letter, there seems to have been a cooling in devotion to these saints. Antagonism has been expressed toward the martyrs themselves and there has been "alienation" between the respective devotees of Kateri and of the martyrs at Auriesville and Fonda (Vecsey 1997: 108). Georges Sioui has recalled his own childhood experiences among the Sisters of Perpetual Help at Lorette, remembering the martyrs' lives couched as a cultural indictment (Sioui 2000:xvi). Nor does he seem to have been alone in this view. A manuscript in the Regis College Archives describes a wary initial reaction of Indians to the martyrs' beatification in the 1920s—though it also attests that these sentiments were eventually overcome:

The Beatification of the Canadian martyrs furnished additional fuel to their devotion. At first it was not well received for want of proper information. The Indians took offence at the pictures showing the sufferings and cruel death of white men at the hands of Indians: it was a reproach cast on their race. They could not see why some Hurons, who had suffered martyrdom as well as the missionaries, did not receive the same honor. But finally the spirit of the faith enlighted [sic] by more knowledge, prevailed and the feast became very popular. (Fr J. Paquin SJ, quoted in J. R. Miller 1996:205)

Perhaps such objections could be partially answered by the advancement of the causes of the Indian confessors and martyrs from St. Francis Xavier du Sault who have been frequently included in hagiographies of Tekakwitha, namely Catherine Gandeaktena who was among the founders of the mission and the Iroquois martyrs: Etienne Tegananokoa, Françoise Gonannhatenha, Marguerite Garongouas, and Etienne Haonhouentsiontaouet. Three of the Iroquois martyrs were included in the Cause of Canonization of the Martyrs of the United States, which was formally submitted in 1941 to the Sacred Congregation of Rites in Rome (Powers 1957:71). But little on their behalf seems to have been done since that time.

More extensive study will be necessary regarding to what extent private devotion to these pious souls existed within the missions, but a few salient facts can be noted. Seven years after Gandeaktena's death, there was a dispute between the Iroquois and the French over her relics (*Positio*:164), and two of the Iroquois martyrs' stories were included in the Algonquin *Ocki Mino Masinaigans* (Cuoq 1893:111ff.).

+ Other Sacraments +

Baptism

The structure of the Algonquian and Iroquoian languages posed a particular theological difficulty in the formula of Baptism. At the heart of this difficulty was how to recast the Latin formula in a way that was sacramentally valid, theologically orthodox, and grammatically correct. Recourse to a European language like Latin or French certainly would get around the entire problem, and this solution was sometimes resorted to. But there evidently must have been a value in continuing to use Algonquian and Iroquoian languages for Baptism, notwithstanding the difficulties involved, for the practice continued.

In St. Jean de Brébeuf's *Relation* of 1636, he addresses his superior Father Paul le Jeune as follows:

> A relative noun with them [the Hurons] includes always the meaning of one of the three persons of the possessive pronoun, so that they can not say simply, Father, Son, Master, Valet, but are obliged to say one of the three, my father, thy father, his father....On this account, we find ourselves hindered from getting them to say properly in their language, *In the name of the Father, and of the Son, and of the holy Ghost.* Would you judge it fitting, while waiting a better expression, to substitute instead, *In the name of our Father, and of his Son, and of their holy Ghost?* Certainly it seems that the three Persons of the most holy Trinity would be sufficiently

43

expressed in this way, the third being in truth the holy Spirit of the first and of the second; the second being Son of the first; and the first, our Father, in the terms of the Apostle, who applies to him those fitting words in Ephesians 3. It may be added that our Lord has given example of this way of speaking, not only in the Lord's Prayer, as we call it from respect to him, but by way of commandment to Mary Magdalaine in saint John 20. to bear from him these beautiful words to his Brethren or Disciples, *I ascend to my Father and to yours*. Would we venture to employ it thus until the Huron language shall be enriched, or the mind of the Hurons opened to other languages? We will do nothing without advice. (JR 10:119-121)

Protestant missionaries had similar difficulties. David Brainerd observed among the Delaware that "Their language does not admit of their speaking any word denoting relation, such as, father, son, &c. *absolutely*; that is, without prefixing a pronoun-passive to it, such as *my, thy, his*, &c. Hence they cannot be baptized in their own language in the name of *the* Father, and *the* Son, &c.; but they may be baptized in the name of Jesus Christ and *his* Father, &c." (Dwight 1822: 336)

And the necessity of adding a referent also apparently caused problems at the end of the formula. Around 1681, Fr. Vaillant taught a dogique in the Mohawk country how to baptize "in our Language, because The Iroquois Tongue has no expression that correctly renders *In nomine*" (JR 62:239).

Brebeuf's and Brainerd's addition of pronominal prefixes was not the only solution that was offered. A particularly interesting passage in Vetromile's *Indian Good Book* gives the baptismal formulas in use among the Passamaquoddy, Penobscot, Micmac, and Montagnais, which he then back-translated into English. Here, the actual words Father and Son were substituted for something of a circumlocution:

Thou child, thee I baptize (wash with water) in the name of Him who has a Son, and of Him who has a Father, and of the Good Spirit. The Micmac say: "In the name of the Spirit that has a Son, and of the Spirit that has a Father, and of the Good Spirit." The Montagnais add one to the third Person, saying: "And of one Good Spirit." (Vetromile 1858a:413)

This was not Vetromile's own formulation, but one that apparently went back to the original missionaries among the Eastern Algonquians. Nonetheless, it raised a few eyebrows among others within the Church, including Vetromile's own ecclesiastical superior, as he revealed in a letter to Fr. J. M. Finotti in 1875:

The Bishop wanted me to alter the form of Baptism in Indian, but I declined for the respect of that old formula, and the more I learned the Indian language, the more I found it to be correct, and now I do not think it could be put in better Indian. I do not know of any language of my knowledge, the Greek and Latin included, that could express the form of baptism in a theological point of view as well as the Indian does. (Pilling 1891:557)

Doubtless this disagreement with his bishop and perhaps others, was the reason that Vetromile included in his *Indian Good Book* a lengthy *apologia* on this manner of baptism, grounding his arguments not only in linguistics but also in long-standing tradition among the tribes in question.

These forms of baptism might, at first sight, appear strange, and not without reason, as they have puzzled, and do yet puzzle a great many who entertain doubts about the validity of the baptism conferred in this manner. This question is continually proposed to us: "Have the Indians, in their language, words corresponding to the following: Father, Son, and Holy Ghost?" Yes, they have them, but to use them under

45

that grammatical form in which they are construed by the English, they would give a formula of baptism, not in Indian, but in English, with Indian words. The Indian form of baptism must be according to the genius of the Indian, and not of the European dialects. It is not our intention to make here a dissertation on languages, but we desire only to lay a few remarks, in order to vindicate a form of baptism, such as we find it preserved amongst the Indians—made by their first missionaries, sanctioned by their successors, and which we do not feel prepared to alter. (Vetromile 1858a:413-414)

Whether Vetromile's position was correct from the standpoint of sacramental theology is not a subject that can be discussed here, though he lays out a quite fascinating case in that regard as well:

> The word father expresses a person that either has
> . or had children, and by itself does not tell how many
> children he has or had, nor when he had them. So
> with the word Son. But the Indian word Wenemanit
> expresses the person *actu* generating the son, one in
> number, and *actu* existing. The word Wemiktankusit
> expresses a person *actu* generated from the existing
> father. Niweskwit means Spirit in substance, the same
> of the other two persons, but distinct from them by
> the addition of uli (*bonitas*), to which prefixing the
> particle *wetchi*, they designate that this *uliniweskwit* is
> not by himself, but comes from the other two persons.
> So with three words, Venèmanit [sic], Wemiktankùsit,
> and Wetchiuliniwèskwit, the Indians can express three
> particular persons, substantially one spirit, but really
> distinct from each other, and the manner in which they
> proceed. What language can exhibit all this with three
> words? (ibid, 415-416)

Confession

A few descriptions of the rite of Confession, rather than merely prayers to be used in the sacrament, are found in the catechetical instructions in the *Indian Good Book*. The priest's prayers are not given—doubtless these were simply done in Latin according to the standard ritual—but formulas for the penitents are listed in the various Indian languages. They are all very similar, and the fullest description comes from the Micmac catechism, of which Vetromile has provided an English translation:

> Q. When one has examined himself well, what has he to do?
> A. He goes to the Patriarch, kneels down, joins the hands, and does four things.
> First: he makes the sign of the Cross, and says, "My Father, pray for me, for I have sinned." Second: He says, "I confess to the Great Spirit, &c. ... through my fault." (Then he stops there). Third: He says to the Patriarch the time that he confessed last, and mentions the sins that he forgot in the last Confession. Fourth: He says all his sins, and in saying them he must show that he is sorry.
> Q. What else?
> A. Then he says, "My Father, I do not remember any thing else; also, I accuse myself of all the sins that I remember, and of all the sins that I do not remember; I beg our Owner to forgive me, and I will perform the penance that you will give to me;" therefore I beseech Mary, &c

Confirmation

The Micmac formula for confirmation is given in the Micmac Catechism in the *Indian Good Book* (p. 388). The accompanying English translation is as follows:

Q. How does the Bishop confirm?

A. He extends his hands over those who are to be confirmed, and he prays to the Good Spirit.

Q. What else?

A. He anoints with holy oil the forehead of each one, in the form of a cross; he gives a little blow on the face, and he says: I mark thee with the cross, and I confirm thee with holy oil, in the name of the Father, and of the Son, and of the Good Spirit. Peace be with thee.

Matrimony

Vetromile's *Indian Good Book* gives the marriage formula in Penobscot as follows—it is interesting primarily because it was used for the bridegroom and bride alike, with no differentation as to sex:

Formula of marriage, which in Indian language
answers for both interrogations.

Q. Kia. N. N. Kenespiulànme kulitahanmannawa kadawi keniswieque whua N. N.?

Q. Thou N. N. dost thou swear to be willing to have for thy consort N. N.?

A. N'uleldahàmen.

A. I do.

The actual matrimonial formula does not seem to be preserved in the *Kaiatonsera Teieriwakwatha*, but this book does give the chants for the Nuptial Mass. In a welcome example of liturgical continuity, one of the hymns given there, *Ise Iesos Sewenniio*, is still very popular at weddings at Akwesasne. The Smithsonian recently featured a rendition of this hymn by Mohawk vocalist and organist Kathleen Thompson on a 2004 CD "Beautiful Beyond: Christian Songs in Native Languages."

Extreme Unction

Prayers for Viaticum and Extreme Unction are given in the *Micmac Paroissien* (Valigny 1912:249–272); of these only the *Pax huic domini* at the beginning of Viaticum is given in Latin, and the rest of the text is in Micmac. Not all of the text of the liturgy is given, so it is likely that the priest's prayers would have been in Latin according to the Roman Rirual. The Micmac portions in this book seem to be reserved for the responses of the sick person, such as the Confiteor and for explanatory notes.

+ The Divine Office +

The earliest accounts of Vespers in the missions show the Indians participating in the hours chanted by their missionaries. Later on, with the advent of dedicated missions and well-established communities of Christian Indians, we begin to see evidence of vernacular services that are called "Vespers" even though they did not always conform to the official Roman texts. Almost certainly these offices were solely for the laity, and resident priests and religious would have continued to say the authorized breviary that was mandated of them. Fr. Jean Enjalran mentions one such service for the laity among the residents of St. Ignace, the Huron and Algonquin mission of Michilimackinac:

> The Christians assemble twice again during the day. In one of these hours, they are made to chant a sort of Vespers, in which the singing is interrupted by short instructions. The non-Christians assist at these Vespers. There is also a special time for assembling the children. (JR 61:107)

A more extensive account from 1677 describes one of these Indian Vespers at the mission of St. Francis Xavier du Sault. It is worth reprinting in full, as it shows how a fusion had been effected between the official Roman liturgy and those Christian prayers which were already a part of the people's devotional life:

> At three o'clock in the afternoon, the bell rings for vespers, for which there are two rows of seats on both sides of the church, from the altar to the lower end of the chapel, whereon the savages sit — the men on one side, and the women on the other. While they take their

51

places, the Father, the Dogique, and two little choir-boys put on their surplices, on the epistle side; and then all four advance to the middle of the altar, where the Father stands with one of the little savage boys, on each side, and the Dogique behind him. All four make the genuflections before the Blessed Sacrament; and at the same time, all the people standing up, the Dogique intones the *Deus in adjutorium* which all sing together, with the *Gloria Patri*. After that, with the Dogique intoning all the psalms, they sing the Vespers in two choirs, all standing up at each *Gloria Patri*, — with which all their psalms conclude, as ours do, — and remaining seated the rest of the time. The psalms are taken from their prayers, which the Father has selected and has set to the principal modes of church music. These prayers are: first, the prayer that they say at rising and at retiring, sung in the 8th mode; second, the prayer for the elevation, in the 1st mode; third, the prayer to the guardian angel, in the 4th; fourth, the thanksgiving for the faith, in the 1st; fifth, the commandments of God, to the air of the *In Exitu*. After that they sing the hymn to the air of the *Iste confessor*, then the *Ave Maria* in the 8th mode, instead of the *Magnificat*; then the orison, with the versicle before it, — to which all respond, as at the end, "'Amen." After Vespers, there is Benediction, so that the sun has set by the time that all is finished; and thus the Father keeps his savages in practice, and makes them spend the entire Sunday devoutly; and the same is done on every feast-day. (JR 60:281-285)

The overall structure of the service is very similar to the traditional Roman Vespers, in beginning with the *Deus in adjutorium* and *Gloria Patri*, followed by five prayers each concluded with a *Gloria Patri*, a hymn, a Marian prayer, and an orison with versicle. There are significant differences in the actual prayers though: the five psalms from the Vulgate have been replaced by five composed prayers, the text of the *Iste Confessor* seems to be replaced by a composed hymn, and the *Ave Maria* is used instead of the *Magnificat*.

This pattern—a service patterned after Vespers but where other texts were substituted for the psalms—continued to prevail at many of the missions even several hundred years later.

A manuscript in the Archives of the Seminary of Quebec, written for Lake of the Two Mountains in 1755, has a Mohawk service titled in French: "Vespers, or Profession of Faith, on the articles of the Catechism." Five lessons follow arranged like psalms, followed by the hymn *Aude Benigne Conditor* in various tones for the liturgical seasons, another hymn for the feasts, the *Magnificat*, and then the *Dominus Vobiscum*, the prayer, and the *Benedicamus Domino* (Anonymous 1755:42 ff.).

The Vespers in the *Kaiatonsera Teieriwakwatha* were apparently originally produced for St. Regis by Fr. Francis Xavier Marcoux but modified for St Francis Xavier du Sault by Nicholas Victor Burtin (Pilling 1888:113). Some of the "psalms" here match those in the catechetical Vespers service of Lake of the Two Mountains mentioned above.

In the *Book of the Seven Nations*, Vespers (*Iokarenre* in Mohawk—"close of day" according to Cuoq 1882) begins with the *Deus in Adjutorium* and the *Gloria Patri*, but the psalms are either composed prayers or other texts like the tract *Nunc Dimittis*, though like true Vespers, each text ends with the *Gloria Patri*. The service ends with its proper *Magnificat*. The *Niina Aiamie Masinaigan* begins with the *Deus in Adjutorium*, followed by 17 "psalms" (again not true psalms), and 19 hymns, after which it lists the four anthems *Alma Redemptoris*, *Ave Regina Cœlorum*, *Regina Cœli*, and *Salve Regina*, one of which was chosen according to the season. Vespers also are composed prayers in the *Aiamie Kushkushkutu Mishinaigan* for the Montagnais.

The Penobscot Vespers in Vetromile's *Good Book* are somewhat strange. There is a wholly vernacular service listed first, but it has only one prayer, the *Paskwe Ahiamihan*, for the psalms. A service for Latin Vespers follows, and this one has the correct number and selection of psalms. After this is a third Vespers service taken from the Little Office of the Blessed Virgin—with the correct psalms in Latin but ending with the *Ave Maris Stella* and *Memorare* in Penobscot.

The Micmac use, in sharp contrast to all the other uses, shows texts that closely follow the Roman office, using direct translations of the proper psalms. Micmac Vespers in the *Indian Good Book* begin with the opening prayers and verses followed by five true psalms: *Dixit Dominus* (109), *Confitebor Tibi* (110), *Beatus Vir* (111), *Laudate Pueri* (112), and *In Exitu Israel* (113), each followed by the *Gloria Patri*. After these is the *Laudate Dominum Omnes Gentes* (116), then the chapter, hymn, verses and response, and the *Magnificat*; antiphons and prayers are also included for St. Ann. The service for Compline in Micmac begins with the opening prayers, then the psalm *Benedic* (102), with a footnote stating that "the Micmacs usually sing Ps. 102 at the commencement of Complin [sic], and omit Ps. 30". Then follows the *Cum Invocarem* (4), *Qui habitat* (90), *Ecce nunc* (133), the verses, a hymn, the chapter, then the *Nunc Dimittis*, "Elajudmanech", *Salve Regina*, and "Elajudmanech".

Pacifique's *Micmac Paroissien* is unusual in that it gives all the hours of the divine office from Matins to Compline. But perhaps its most notable feature is its copious use of hymns from the Paris Breviary of 1736 (Vintimille 1736), part of a neo-Gallican and Jansensist liturgical reform that once enjoyed widespread use in France but which fell into disrepute by the middle of the 1800s. These hymns include *Die dierum principe* for Matins, *O fons amoris* for Terce, *Jam solis excelsum* for Sext, and *Labente jam solis* for None.

In 1815, the archbishop of Quebec, Joseph Octave Plessis, visited Acadia and noted with consternation that the Abbé Jean Mandé Sigogne (1763–1844), who served the Acadians and the Micmac alike, was using the Parisian breviary as opposed to the Roman one which was the norm in the diocese. When Plessis ordered Sigogne to conform to the diocesan usage, the latter replied that he would rather leave the country (*Dictionary of Canadian Biography* VII:803). No further action was taken against Sigogne, and the use of the neo-Gallican office continued: in 1844 a member of the Micmac choir was singing the Paris breviary's *O*

Dominicâ ad Officium Nocturnum.

[A Septuagesima ad Pascha, loco Alleluia, dicitur : Laus tibi, Dómine, Rex æternæ glóriæ.]

In Dominicis per Adventum, & post Circumcisionem usque ad Præsentationem Domini, vel saltem ad Septuagesimam, (si Septuagesima priùs evenerit,) Officium fit ut notatur in Proprio de Tempore: in aliis verò Dominicis fit ut sequitur.

Invitatorium. Dóminum qui fecit nos, * Veníte adorémus.

Ps. 94.

Psalmus 94.

VEníte, exultémus Dómino : jubilémus Deo salutári nostro : præoccupémus fáciem ejus in confessióne, & in psalmis jubilémus ei.

Dóminum qui fecit nos, * Veníte, adorémus.

Quóniam Deus magnus Dóminus, & Rex magnus super omnes deos : quóniam non repellet Dóminus plebem suam : quia in manu ejus sunt omnes fines terræ, & altitúdines móntium ipse conspícit.

* Veníte, adorémus.

Quóniam ipsíus est mare, & ipse fecit illud, & áridam fundavérunt manus ejus : veníte, adorémus, & procidámus ante Deum : plorémus coram Dómino qui fecit nos, quia ipse est Dóminus Deus noster; nos autem pópulus ejus, & oves páscuæ ejus.

* Veníte, adorémus.

Hódie si vocem ejus audiéritis, nolíte obduráre corda vestra, sicut in exacerbatióne, secundùm diem teptatiónis in deserto, ubi tentavérunt me patres vestri, probavérunt & vidérunt ópera mea.

* Veníte, adorémus.

Quadragínta annis próximus fui generatióni huic, & dixi: Semper hi errant corde; ipsi verò non cognovérunt vias meas : quibus jurávi in ira mea, si introíbunt in réquiem meam.

* Veníte, adorémus.

Glória Patri, & Fílio, & Spirítui sancto : Sicut erat in principio, & nunc, & semper, & in sécula sæculórum. Amen.

Repet. Dóminum qui fecit nos, * Veníte, adorémus.

Hymnus. C.

DIe diérum principe
Christus sepulchri cárcere,
Lux vera mundi, pródiit.

Et mors & horréndum chaos
Vocem jubentis áudiunt :
Nos súrdiores, ò pudor!
Deo pigréer óbsequi?

Umbris sepulta dum stupet
Natúra, lucis fílii
Surgámus, & noctem piis
Exerceámus cánticis.

Legem, prophétas, & sacro
Psalmos caléntes lúmine,
Profána dum silent loca,
Divína templa pérsonent.

Coeléstis hæc vincat tuba
Cordis sopórem lánguidi,
Novíque mores exprimant
Vitam resúrgentis novam.

Hoc consequémur te duce,
Fons caritátis, ò Deus,
Qui jugibus addis líteræ
Visæ datórem Spíritum.

Sit Jesu Patri, laus Fílio;
Par sit tibi laus, Spíritus.

Dominicâ in I. Nocturno.

Afflante quo mentes sacris
Lucent & ardent ignibus. Amen.

IN I. NOCTURNO.

Ant. 3. toni a. Beátus vir.

Asteríscus hic * notat mediationem & pausam.

Psalmus 1.

BEátus vir qui non ábiit in consílio impiórum, & in via peccatórum non stetit, * & in cáthedra pestiléntiæ non sedit :

Sed in lege Dómini volúntas ejus, * & in lege ejus meditábitur die ac nocte.

Et erit tanquam lignum, quod plantátum est secus decúrsus aquárum, * quod fructum suum dabit in témpore suo :

Et fólium ejus non défluet : * & ómnia quæcúmque fáciet prosperabúntur.

Non sic ímpii, non sic : * sed tanquam pulvis quem prójicit ventus à fácie terræ.

Ideo non resúrgent ímpii in judício, * neque peccatóres in concílio justórum :

Quóniam novit Dóminus viam justórum, * & iter impiórum períbit.

Glória Patri, & Fílio, * & Spirítui sancto :

Sicut erat in princípio, & nunc, & semper, * & in sécula sæculórum. Amen.

Hi versùs Glória & Sicut erat, dicuntur in fine Psalmórum, Divisiónum & Canticórum, nisi aliter notetur.

Ant. Beátus vir qui non ábiit in consílio impiórum : sed in lege Dómini meditábitur die ac nocte.

Ant. 4. f. Servíte Dómino.

Psalmus 2.

QUare fremuérunt gentes, * & pópuli meditáti sunt inánia?

Astitérunt reges terræ, & príncipes convenérunt in unum * adversùs Dóminum & adversùs Christum ejus.

Dirumpámus víncula eórum, * & projiciámus à nobis jugum ipsórum.

Qui hábitat in coelis irridébit eos, * & Dóminus subsannábit eos.

Tunc loquétur ad eos in ira sua,* & in furóre suo contúrbabit eos.

Ego autem constitútus sum Rex ab eo super Sion montem sanctum ejus, * prædicans præcéptum ejus.

Dóminus dixit ad me : * Fílius meus es tu, ego hódie génui te.

Póstula à me, & dabo tibi gentes hereditátem tuam, * & possessiónem tuam términos terræ.

Reges eos in virga férrea, * & tanquam vas fíguli confrínges eos.

Et nunc, reges, intellígite : * erudímini, qui judicátis terram.

Servíte Dómino in timóre : * & exsultáte ei cum tremóre.

Apprehéndite disciplínam, nequando irascátur Dóminus, * & pereátis de via justa.

Cùm exárserit in brevi ira ejus,* beáti omnes qui confídunt in eo.

Ant. Servíte Dómino, & exhilátee ei. Apprehéndite disciplínam.

Ant. 8. G. Dicant.

Psalmus 3.

DOmine, quid multiplicáti sunt qui tríbulant me? multi insúrgunt adversùm me.

Multi dicunt ánimæ meæ; *

A ij

---

338   AGANTIEOIMGEOEL

tetli nenemitip nteligen ag tan
tetli nemitotip tellogoap. * Tjogoitag...
. Neoinsgegipong°g pemi ogoai-
ogtagapenig o°gela, eiep : oage-
la ogoamlamonoal nantemi gioó-
oigel, gegtog mo nenemitigol
ntaotil tan eltegel ; na oetji mel-
gapogoap oegaianel, ma gisi
pisgoetatiog noant°gôtimig tog.
Gsagmamino...

    Tan teli gpmi... metj....*
Tjogoitag.... Gsagmamino....

HYMNE

Die dierum principe

NAGOEG taneg ansema temgeoeieg tlisip pegenigtog oetj-

AGTATPAG   339

asigsepeneg oasôgoegeg; elp na
pa Glist lnog ogetli pagtatene-
moan otgotaganigtog lamalgeg
oetji otalgalesitj gisi tli nsogoni-
singeg.

Npoagan ag sespi magtaoa-
mog netaoi gelistemoatitjel Gi-
°olgol gelosilitjel ; gino sgato pe-
tjili gepistaganatigo, agai nagatj-
oltigo gtangistemoaneno Gtjinis-
gam gelolnogo.

Esg mset gôgoel peigoi pgenig-
tog tetlisoltigel telegel, gino sgato oasôgoegigtog oetji otjigoltigo
tôg nemtjitanetj, ag na tepgig
tan tetotgig mao atignetemenetj

Neo-Gallican hymn for Matins, *Die Dierum Principe*, which first appeared in the Parisian Breviary of 1736 (top) and was still included in Fr. Pacifique's *Micmac Paroissien* of 1912 (bottom) despite having been eradicated in France by that time.

luce qui mortalibus during Vespers (Boudreau 1996). The date of 1875 is commonly given for the extinction of the neo-Gallican uses, when the last diocese in France to use one, Orléans, abandoned it for the Roman rite. Yet as the *Micmac Paroissien* attests to their continued survival in the Canadian missions into the early 1900s, a reappraisal of the final stages of neo-Gallicanism in the Americas would perhaps be in order.

+ Music and Hymnody +

> *Indian singing is slow, solemn and affecting. It is not art, but the heart that sings. Their singing is more suitable for divine service and more soul-elevating than that we hear in many of our large churches, with their "sharps and flats" and their endless and senseless repetitions. Indian singing inspires and promotes devotion. Would to God that this could be said of all our church singing!*
>
> —Fr. Chrysostom Veruyst, 1900 (Veruyst 1900:59)

That the Indians showed remarkable ability in singing sacred music is attested quite often by the missionaries, such as in a 1676 letter of Fr. Jean Enjalran from Sillery:

> One is charmed to hear the various choirs, which the men and the women form in order to sing during mass and at vespers. The nuns of France do not sing more agreeably than some savage women here; and, as a class, all the savages have much aptitude and inclination for singing the hymns of the Church, which have been rendered into their language. (JR 60:145)

Among the styles of music in which the Indians particularly excelled was plainchant or Gregorian Chant. Vetromile's 1858 *Ahiamihewintuhangan: The Prayer Song* gives an intriguing glimpse into both the theoretical and practical aspects of plainchant among the Abenaki at Old Town. The book opens with a preface that throws a sociological light on the Penobscot's preference for plainchant:

> The native Americans have a natural disposition to
> music.... The rules of Harmony being too complicated
> for them, and the strict mathematical division of time
> in modern music, retarding the spontaneous expression
> of their heart, account for the preference that they give
> to melody above harmony, and to the Gregorian Chant
> above the Figured Song. The solemnity of Church-
> music suits the Indians, who are generally grave even
> to sadness, and who have none of the giddy vivacity
> peculiar to some nations of Europe, and who despise
> it.
>
> For a number of years I have tried to introduce among
> them some masses and hymns of modern music, but
> without success. Hence, setting aside the Figured-song,
> I resolved to cultivate among them only the Plain-chant,
> and something of the Broken-chant, (cantus fractus.)
> (Vetromile 1858b:v–vi)

Following the preface is a section "An Abridgement of the
Gregorian Chant", which is a primer on the singing of chant,
intended "to give some practical instructions on Church-music, in
order to aid the native Americans to sing the praises of the Lord
according to the different rites of the Catholic Church." It includes
descriptions and examples of the clefs, note values, and scales as
well as the intonations of the Psalms in Latin. The intended use
of this volume was probably for the members of the Abenaki
singing school conducted by "three able Indians": Salomon
Swassin, Sapiel Sakalexis and Misel Nicolas. Swassin (d. 1862) is
himself an interesting example of native Catholicism's important
contributions to the Anglo-American Church at large, in that he
proudly served as the founding choirmaster and instructor at the
church of St. Michael's in the city of Bangor, Maine.

Vetromile's attestation of the Indians' preference for Gregorian
chant is well reflected in the mission books, and examples of chant
in the native languages abound. There are over 80 pages of it in the
Book of Seven Nations and over 60 pages in the *Aiamie Kushkushkutu
Mishinaigan*. The *Kaiatonsera Teieriwakwatha* devotes most of its over

A - ne - hel - da - ma - wi - nè.
Tchiksdaweminè eli wilikudmolek.
K'te - man-gu - el - mi - nè.

MASS ALLA PASTORALE—FOR CHRISTMAS NIGHT.

Kyrie.

Zezus Ketemanghelminè, Zezus Ketemanghelminè,

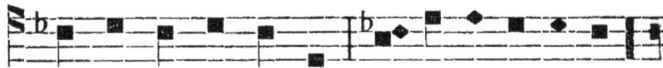

Zezus Ketemanghelminè, Ke - te-manghelminè.

Nixkam, Nixkam, Nixkam, Ke- te-manghelmi-nè,

Zezus Kete - manghelminè, Kete - manghelminè,

Ke - te - man-ghel-mi-nè.

Gloria.

Chorus.

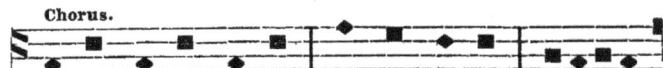

Aghim, aghim, .aghim, K'tankam-i-kook u - le-

A page from Vetromile's *Ahiamihewintuhangan; The Prayer Song* (1858), showing the beginning of the Mass for Christmas Night.

400 pages to chant, and there are many extant manuscripts which contain chants as well.

Vetromile's experience concerning the figured song among the Abenaki was not universal. A vast body of vernacular hymnody has been preserved from the missions of the Northeast, and most of the mission books indeed have pages and pages of translated hymns. Most of the sources give the texts alone, without any music; sometimes, as in the *Book of Seven Nations*, a notation will say that the words should be sung to the tune of a pre-existing French hymn, but many times even this designation is absent.

Hymnody was generally retained for those parts of the Mass where vernacular plainchant was still prohibitively difficult to implement: such as for the complicated system of Roman Propers. Of course, hymns sung during the traditional High Mass were not liturgical *per se* in that they were not standardized by the Missal. Nonetheless, sóme standardization is suggested by the mission paroissiens, where certain hymns are listed for certain feasts. Doubtless the order and usage were not fixed absolutely; in fact, for some feasts there seem to be more hymns listed than can be reasonably sung in a single Mass. And perhaps deviations from what was laid out in the paroissiens were quite common, but overall there does seem to be more fixity to the hymnody in the liturgies than is typical today.

One particular hymn originating from the missions deserves special notice, as it has enjoyed a widespread fame: the "Huron Carol" ascribed to St. Jean de Brébeuf: *Jesous Ahatonhia* or *Jesous Ahatonnia*. This composition has been republished in a number of hymn and Christmas carol compliations, particularly in Canada, and it is now even found in a number of Protestant hymnals. The most popular version is probably the English *'Twas in the moon of wintertime* done by Jesse Middleton in 1926, which, however, is more of a paraphrase than a true translation of either the original Huron or the French translation of Paul Tsa8enhohi found in the *Collection of Huron Songs*. Middelton's rendering has been criticized not only for its liberties with the text but also particularly for its romanticized reimagining of an Indian Christmas story: the shepherds are "hunter braves", the Magi are "chiefs" who bring gifts of "fox and beaver pelt", and God is Ojibwe *Gitchi manitou* "Great Spirit" rather than the normal Huron transliteration *Dï8* from French *Dieu* = "God". But such critiques have not dulled the popularity of the Middleton translation among either whites or Indians, and it has even been recently rendered into Micmac and recorded by the Eskasoni trio (Various artists 2001).

There are less examples in the missions for forms other than plainchant and hymnody, but these are not absent either. Vetromile's quote above shows that the *cantus fractus* was being used by the Abenaki in the mid-1800s, and later in the same book he gives a Credo in broken-chant "alla Palestrina", although this is in Latin and not the vernacular. However, Fr. Clement McNaspy attests to rather full range of vernacular polyphony among the Mohawk at St. Francis Xavier du Sault:

> At present the liturgical music library of Caughnawaga Mission includes almost all the Gregorian masses and dozens of modern masses of all schools, arranged in Iroquois and handsomely multicopied. In addition there are hundreds of motets (classic polyphonic and modern) and the Gregorian Propers for all Sundays, commons, and greater feasts, all in the same vernacular arrangements. In terms of sheer bulk and quality this represents one of the most useful collections of sacred music in Canada: yet all had to be done by hand and is the result of years of painstaking adaptation. (McNaspy 1947).

+ Other Characteristic Devotions +

Rosaries and Chaplets

The Dominican Rosary was an extremely popular devotion in the missions. We find the following pious custom in the mission of the Atticameg in the early 1650s:

> Some time ago, when the Christians of this place died, their rosaries were buried with them. Last year, this custom was changed into a still more holy one, on the occasion of the death of a good Christian woman who, in dying, gave her rosary to another, begging her to keep it and to say it for her, at least on holy days. This act of charity was promised to her; and that custom has been introduced since that time,—so that, when any one dies, his rosary is presented, with some little gift, to some person selected among the company, who undertakes to carry it and to say it for the soul of the deceased, at least on Feast-days and Sundays. (JR 37:49)

Yet other chaplets were quite popular as well. Fr. Chauchetiere provides us with a sampling of those that were current at St. Francis Xavier du Sault in 1682:

> There is a savage woman who says the Rosary fully twenty times a Day; and another who says it six times in her day, by dividing it in a very ingenious fashion. They find out all their devotions by themselves, for

63

they call one Rosary that "of the five wounds;" another, "the Rosary of the ten virtues of the blessed virgin," as the blessed Jeanne invented it; another, "The rosary of twelve beads," invented by sister Margueritte du st. Sacrement, a Carmelite; another, "The chaplet of St. Joseph;" and all these are recited while they are going to or returning from their fields. (JR 62:181)

The above chaplets all had a European origin, but two other ones can be considered more distinctively Canadian. The chaplet of the Confraternity of the Holy Family dates from the establishment of that society (see page 81). We have documented evidence of it being said by Catherine Gandeaktena, and it was among the devotions that Kateri and Marie-Therese made a part of their Saturday penance (*Positio*:160). The chaplet was made with 3 large beads separating 3 sets of 10 small beads, and the accompanying prayers as given in the *Book of Seven Nations* are in three decades as follows:

		(a meditation)
repeat 3x	1x	*Our Father...*
	repeat 10x	*V. Jesus, Mary, Joseph, Joachim, Anne, come to our assistance.* *R. God the Holy Trinity, have mercy on us.*
	1x	*Glory Be...*

But unquestionably the chaplet with the most authentically native pedigree was Catherine's Chaplet. In Fr. Claude Chauchetière's *Life of the Blessed Catherine Tegakoüita*, which he wrote probably around 1685, he noted that the devotion was already in use by Francis Tsonnatouan, a friend of Kateri's, shortly after the blessed's death:

> He had a portrait with him and some relics around his neck. He also had around his neck a little chaplet that he called "Catherine's chaplet," which was composed of a Credo that he said on the cross, a Pater and an Ave

Map of the Rosary, from Vetromile's *Indian Good Book* (1858a).

which are strung with the cross, and three other small
beads which are three Glorias, and he said this chaplet
to give thanks to the Holy Trinity for the graces that
had been bestowed to Catherine. (Chauchetière 1887:
144-145; translation mine)

Chauchetière confirmed its wider use a decade later and also
mentioned his invention of the devotion in a letter he sent to Fr.
Jacques Jouheneau on September 20, 1694:

I beg the Reverend father rector of the novitiate to
have his novices say a "pater," an "ave," and the "gloria
patri" three times for me. This is a devotion practiced
here among the Savages and the French, who go to the
tomb of Catherine, who is interred in the church of the
Sault, when they wish to obtain some favor from God. I
began it on the very day of her burial; and I have always
believed that it was she who at the end of the year saved
me, when our chapel was blown down by the storm.
(JR 64:155)

These prayers are still very much at the heart of the cult of Blessed
Kateri, and to this day, prayer cards and documents in support of
her canonization still call for the same set of one Our Father, one
Hail Mary, and three Glory Be's.

Devotional Wampum

*Receive, O Lady of Heaven, this present, offered to you by
the chosen ones of your Huron Servants. It is a collar full
of hidden meaning. It is composed of our finest pearls. It
is inspired and enriched by the utterance and the greeting
given you of old by the Angel Gabriel. We have nothing more
precious in our hands, and nothing holier in our hearts, for
presenting to you, and for gaining us the kingdom of Heaven*

through your mediation.
>> *—offering of a wampum belt made by the Hurons
to the Virgin, 1654 (JR 41:175)*

Wampum is often popularly, but not quite accurately, conceived of as Indian money, though to be sure, it was a valued object in native culture and had economic value. In the *Jesuit Relation* of 1677–1678, Father Enjalran at the Huron mission at Michilimackinac makes note of wampum offerings accompanying the *pain benit* at the Mass:

> The Christians take turn in furnishing the blessed bread every Sunday at Mass, together with 33 porcelain beads, in order to unite their offering with that which Jesus Christ makes; and he who has presented the blessed bread goes afterward to hand to all assisting one of their plates of bark, in which a few beads of porcelain or colored glass are dropped by each, according to his means and devotion. (JR 61:107)

Yet wampum to the Eastern Woodland tribes meant far more than merely a medium of exchange. It had a profound cultural significance and played a prominent and very symbolic part in some of the most vital business of the state. Its use is not very ancient; it is found only rarely in archaeological sites before the 1600s. Nonetheless, accounts of the 1600s and 1700s are filled with references to what in the French sources were generally called "porcelain" and "porcelain collars". These were used in treaty negotiations, condolence ceremonies, record keeping, and other important activities of the Eastern Woodland villages—in a very real sense, wampum was the preferred instrument of diplomacy (Tooker 1978).

It is, therefore, no surprise that Christian Indians adapted this practice to the service of their religion. In the mid-1650s, the Huron mission on the island of Orléans received charitable donations from the members of the Congregation of Our Lady in the professed house of the Jesuits in Paris. Touched by their generosity, the Hurons decided to return the favor with a gift of their own, and asked Fr. Pierre-Joseph Chaumonot (1611-1693) to write an accompanying thank-you letter in Huron and French. Within this letter is a description of how the idea of devotional wampum was born:

> Several years ago, you sent us some rich presents. We met together and said, 'What shall we send to those noble servants of the Virgin? They need nothing from us,' said we, 'for they are rich; but they love the mother of Jesus; so let us send them a collar of our Porcelain, whereon is written the greeting that an Angel from Heaven brought to the Virgin.' We have recited as many rosaries, in the space of two months, as there are beads in the collar—one bead of black porcelain being worth two of white. Present this collar to her, and tell her that we wish to honor her. (JR 41:171)

Wampum was bestowed not only to French churches but between mission churches as well. In 1677, the Hurons at Lorette sent a wampum belt to their fellow Christians at St. Francis Xavier du Sault "encouraging them to accept the faith in good earnest, and to build a chapel as soon as possible; and it also exhorted them to combat the various demons who conspired for the ruin of both missions" (JR 63:193). The Iroquois at St. Francis Xavier promptly hung the belt on a beam above the altar in their chapel, and this may be the same belt that was preserved at Kahnawake into the 20th century (see picture on the following page), but which seems to have been stolen.

With both the Paris church and the Sault mission, the Huron's grant of wampum seems to have served as a visible bond of Christian alliance and ecclesiastical communion. But it was also used within the mission in a strictly devotional manner. At the establishment of Ancienne Lorette in 1673, the Huron employed wampum to invoke the prayers of angels and saints:

An old photograph of a now lost wampum belt once kept at St. Francis Xavier du Sault in Kahnawake. This belt is thought to be the same one given to the mission by the Lorette Hurons in 1677. From *Historic Caughnawaga* (Devine 1922).

But, before leaving Notre Dame de Foye, they all went on a pilgrimage to Sillery for a general communion, and to make a public vow in honor of saint Michael, the patron of that place. They presented a collar of porcelain beads to that glorious archangel, to obtain through his intercession a successful establishment in the new village of Lorette. They were hardly lodged there when they made another vow and another communion in honor of saint Anne. To her they likewise offered a collar of porcelain beads, to ask from her the grace of seeing before long, in the middle of their village, the house of the Blessed Virgin, her daughter (JR 58:147-149).

The weaving of devotional wampum belts was not merely a form of artistic expression or thanksgiving, but was a kind of physical prayer which began with the devotions of the faithful:

I will say that these good members of the Congregation have adopted a pious practice of making a little present every Sunday to the Virgin, each one giving a porcelain bead for each rosary recited during the week. The number of these beads,—which are the pearls of the country,—runs sometimes as high as seven or eight hundred; and their devotion has prompted them to make collars of these in the style of embroidery,—in which, interweaving beads of violet and white porcelain, they write what they wish to say in honor of the Virgin. (JR 41:165)

There was certainly a ceremonial dimension to wampum as well. At the mission of the Algonquins at Michilimackinac, a sacrilege committed against the cross prompted the Christian Kiskakons to offer atonement for the sin with a wampum belt. They presentated this gift in a formal ceremony that blended Catholic liturgical practice with the language and rituals of traditional Eastern

Woodland diplomacy:

> Father Nouvel, vested in surplice and preceded by the Cross, as on the day of the insult, went and knelt down at the foot of the Cross, together with the Christians. The elders and young men, of every nation, stood around the Cross; some Christian Hurons were there moreover, with Father Pierçon. They remained for some time, kneeling at the foot of the Cross in silence. Then the Captain of the Kiskakons, holding the Collar in his hand, addressed Jesus Christ, the missionaries, and all the nations assembled, with wonderful energy, and in sentiments of truly Christian piety: 'Thou sawest us from the highest heaven' (said he) 'O Jesus Christ, when those who have no sense did injury to thy Cross; and thou didst regard us with an indignant eye. Look now with a favorable eye upon our atonement, by which we desire to efface all the evil that we have done.' After commending to him all their children,—who are the ones in whom alone they seem to interest themselves,—and after exhorting all to obey Jesus Christ and the fathers who are his spokesmen, he addressed himself to us, praying us to continue to take charge of them, as we had heretofore done; while they protested that it was their will to hear and obey us. Having finished his discourse, he placed his collar over the two arms of the Crucifix, which a young savage held erect. The other nations spoke conformably to what the chief had just said, thanking him for the amends that he had just offered to Jesus Christ for all, and exhorting all in a similar manner to obedience and respect for the Cross (JR 61:143–145)

Overall, far from being an example of merely artistic inculturation, the Christian use of wampum had a distinctly devotional cast. The physical value of the gift was not meant to stand alone but was meant as a concrete, visible symbol of an interior disposition. It was not only valuable beads that the Hurons were offering to

Christ or to Archangel Michael, St. Anne, or the Virgin, but prayers, devotions, and the honor due to the perfected Christians in heaven. Analogies could also be drawn between the wampum weavers and the icon writers of the Eastern churches whose process is as much a religious devotion as an art form.

Prayer Sticks

The Eastern Woodland Indians did not have a system of written language until after contact with Europeans. Nonetheless, they did make use of written pictographs on birchbark or wood to maintain records and to aid the memory in the recitation of religious rites or narratives (see images on page 75).

With the introduction of Christianity, this practice of using pictographic mnemonic aids was simply adapted by catechumens to the doctrines and devotions of the new religion, as in this example from among the Montagnais in the 1720s:

> The men make use, to a certain extent, of artificial aids to memory. One of them, in order to learn the *Veni Creator* in his language, made some small figures for himself on a piece of bark for each verse, which reminded him of the meaning of each strophe. I saw by accident in his curious writing, at the *hostem repellas longius*, a sort of little imp, which reminded him of the versicle: *Matchi-manitoû*, etc., "the evil spirit, our enemy." Another astonished me last year. Before making his confession for Easter, he prepared himself and examined his conscience; and at each of his sins he cut a notch on a small stick. By referring to this stick, which answered for a book, he hesitated but once with regard to the number of and the circumstances attending the sins committed during the year, of which he accused himself, Everything of that kind seems spiritual to him who associates with and loves men of that sort. I asked myself whether it were St. Ignatius who had taught him this mysterious secret (JR 68:103)

The utility of a pictographic system for instructing the natives in Christianity was not lost on the missionaries. Father Jean Du Quen (1603–1659), at the mission of Tadoussac in the 1640s, faced a vast mission field of nomadic tribes too large for the handful of priests that were available. Du Quen solved the problem by leaving teaching tools in his stead:

> The Father, when obliged to separate from these good Neophytes, left them five Books, or five Chapters of a Book, composed after their manner; these Books were no other than five sticks variously fashioned, in which they are to read what the Father has earnestly inculcated upon them....
>
> These poor people, withdrawing into their forests, usually separate themselves into three bands; the Father has given to the chief of each squad these five Books, or these five Chapters, which contain all that they must do. It is a truly innocent pleasure to see these new Preachers hold these Books or these sticks in one hand, draw forth a stick with the other, and present it to their audience with these words: "Behold the stick or the Massinahigan,"–that is to Say, "the book of the superstitions;" "our Father has written it himself. He tells you that it is only the Priests who can say Mass and hear Confessions; that our drums, our sweatings, and our throbbings of the breast are inventions of the manitou or of the evil spirit, who wishes to deceive us;" and so of all those other Books of wood, which serve them as well as the most gilded volumes of a Royal Library. (JR 29:139 ff.)

Du Quen's five massinahigan each had their own unique purpose and symbolism which the author described more fully:

> The first is a black stick, which is to remind them of the horror that they must have for their innovations and their former superstitions.
>
> The second is a white stick, which marks for them

the devotions and the prayers which they shall say every day, and the manner of offering and presenting to God their minor actions.

The third is a red stick, on which is written that which they are to do on Sundays and Feasts, how they are all to assemble in a great cabin, hold public prayers, sing spiritual Songs, and above all, listen to the one who shall keep these Books or these Sticks, and who will give the explanation of them to the whole assembly.

The fourth is the Book or the stick of punishment, therefore it is wound with little ropes. This Book prescribes the manner of correcting the delinquents with love and charity; to their fervor must be granted what is reasonable, and the excesses to which they are easily inclined must be cut off.

The fifth Book is a stick notched with various marks, which signifies how they are to behave in dearth and in plenty,— the recourse which they must have to God, the thanksgivings that they must render him, and the hope which they must always have in his goodness, especially as regards eternity. (ibid:141)

As Du Quen formulated them, the five types of massinahigan can thus be summarized as black (condemnation), white (devotional), red (liturgical), wound (disciplinary), and notched (homiletic).

When Du Quen saw those tribes again a year later, he found that they had made good use of the materials he left:

The Christians, seeing their Father come, rejoiced; each one gave account of what had happened during the Winter. Those to whom Books of wood had been given,—that is to say, tokens which were to serve as topical memorandums for the Principal persons, that they might instruct the others upon certain of the more important points,—faithfully brought these forward, and, without dissimulating, told quite ingenuously what had been committed contrary to each Chapter or each part of those Books. (JR 31:231–233)

Ah-ton-we-tuck (top) and On-saw-kie (bottom), engravings from original paintings by George Catlin, showing prayer sticks of the Kenekuk religion (Catlin 1866: plates 186 and 189).

The history of these massinahigan has some very striking parallels with the history of the Sahale stick on the Northwest Coast two centuries later. In 1837, Fr. François Norbert Blanchet (1795–1883) and Fr. Modeste Demers (1809–1871) were assigned to the vast region of the Oregon Territory, totaling 375,000 square miles. To assist in the catechesis of the tribes of the area, Blanchet devised a sort of Catholic totem called the Sahale stick on which he marked the various events of salvation history. Its use spread rapidly across the Northwestern tribes and gave rise to a more easily produced paper version called the "Catholic ladder," which figured so prominently in the Oregon territory that thousands were printed for the missions by Pope Pius IX (Vecsey 1997:315).

There does not, however, seem to be any evidence that Du Quen's earlier system, with its particular sequence of colors, was followed by any subsequent missionary or the Indians themselves. Eventually, as the written forms of native languages like Montagnais began to be standardized, and as the members of the tribes themselves began to learn the art of letters, the need for this kind of pictography in the Northeastern missions waned. However, it still continued on in modified form in the Christian Micmac hieroglyphs.

+ Religious Life and Offices +

Since the early colonial era, many Catholics of American Indian blood have entered established congregations of religious life. The first native girl to become a nun was Sister Genevieve-Agnes de Tous-Saints (1642–1657), whose Huron name was Skanudharoua; she made her final vows a few hours before her death from disease. The first native priest seems to have been Fr. James Chrysostom Bouchard (1823–1889), also known as Watomika, born of a Delaware Indian father and French mother and who entered the Society of Jesus in 1856. Abbé Prosper Vincent (1842–1915), or Sawatanin, was a Huron from Lorette, and Fr. Michael Jacobs (1902–1990) or Wishe Karhaienton, was a Mohawk of Kahnawake.

The recent USCCB report *Native American Catholics at the Millennium* found 27 priests, 8 seminarians, 74 deacons, and 34 women religious of Native American descent throughout the United States (USCCB 2002). The United States also currently boasts two bishops of Native ancestry: Archbishop Charles J. Chaput, OFM Cap (b. 1944) of the Archdiocese of Denver, of Potawatomi descent; and Bishop Donald E. Pelotte, SSS (b. 1945) of the Diocese of Gallup, New Mexico, of Abenaki descent.

Natives' participation in the life of the Church over the last 300 years has also resulted in offices and congregations, both formal and informal, that were formed wholly or mostly within the context of the Indian missions.

Dogique

In the early days of the French missions, certain native Christians who proved stalwart in the faith were appointed to fill the office of *dogique*. This term was used in the foreign missions to denote natives who insructed their countrymen, and it derived from the Japanese word *dojiku*, which the Jesuits of Japan used of well-instructed neophytes who were entrusted with catechesis and the care of the community in the missionary's absence (JR 27:311; Campeau 1989:66).

In North America, dogiques served as an important bridge between the priest and the people and functioned as catechists, preachers, prayer leaders, and directors of the singing at Mass and at Vespers. Notable holders of the office included Pierre Atironta (Huron, d. 1672); Waxaway (Abenaki); and Louis Taondechoren (Huron, d. after 1677). A few passages in the *Jesuit Relations* attest to women as dogiques (JR 35:251; 57:53; 62:113). These are described as catechists of women.

Dogiques are first mentioned in a 1644 letter of Jerome Lalemant among the Hurons, where the missionary speaks in no uncertain terms on the indispensable role these natives played in the spread of the Gospel:

> The older Christians...perform the office of Dogique, in the absence of our Fathers. In their wars and on their hunts, even when they are in large bands, they offer public prayers, and hold divine service, as strictly as if they were in their Church; they instruct and baptize, with much satisfaction and edification, in times of danger; the reputation of their virtue pervades the foreign Tribes with whom they trade; they preach there the holiness of the Christian law; they inspire everywhere the desire of enjoying the blessing that they possess, and imperceptibly open the door for us to many great nations who could not hear our name without a shudder, and who had looked upon us in the past only as persons who brought misfortune upon them. (JR 27:67)

A later quotation from Sillery in 1682 elaborates further:

these [unbaptized] the Catechist or dogique seeks in all the Cabins, and assembles them in the Church, to which all come at noon with admirable punctuality. The same catechist teaches the Catechism regularly, every Day, to all the boys in his cabin, and also shows them how to sing the prayers that are chanted in our Church. A woman, on the other hand, does likewise, at the same hour, in her Cabin for all the girls. I have charged a woman Named Jeanne with this duty. (JR 62: 113-115)

Undoubtedly, the native appreciation for and the importance attached to rhetoric made this position a natural fit for elders in the community.

The male dogiques occasionally assumed such roles that might even invite comparison with the ordained permanent diaconate of today. However, their office was by no means a clerical one. Dogiques were simply laymen appointed to their posts, and they were not ordained. Nonetheless, a 1677 letter of Fr. Cholenec describing the practice at St. Francis Xavier du Sault shows how surprisingly prominent of a liturgical role they could play:

On Sunday Morning the Father says Mass at 8 o'clock... After The Gospel, The Father preaches them a sermon, or has one preached to them by the Dogique, who is ever Incomparable in this respect — as he again proved quite recently, on Christmas day. The Father told him on the eve that he would have to preach the following day on the subject of the feast, and said Nothing further to him. Nevertheless, that man preached a very long time, and admirably Explained, in full, everything connected with the mystery of the day, — the journey of the Pregnant Virgin and of st. Joseph, her spouse; Their Entry into Bethlehem; the refusal to admit them into any of the houses; respecting their lodging, and Their taking refuge in The Stable; how the blessed Virgin was delivered there, and everything Else Regarding the Angels, the shepherds, etc., — so that the father himself was astonished, as he has since told me.

After the sermon, the Dogique Intones the *credo* in Their language, in The Church plain-song, and they thus continue Their Chanting Until the end of the mass. (JR 60:279–281)

Later that day the dogique would then vest in surplice along with the priest and the choir-boys and advance to the middle of the altar. There, he would intone the *Deus in Adjutorium* and the psalms for Vespers (see pages 51–52). Giving such liturgical prominence to laymen was certainly unusual before Vatican II, but in Canada and other missions it was no doubt due to the particular difficulties of the Indian missions rather than any progressive concepts of lay leadership. Particularly in the early years of the missions, dogiques would have possessed a fluency in the language and a cultural influence with Indian Catholics that the French Jesuits did not, so their assistance and example would have certainly been invaluable in fledgling Christian communities.

But as time went on, the office which was so prominent in the earliest years waned in importance as the barriers of communication and culture between missionaries and Indians gradually lowered. Yet the concept of native ecclesiastical leaders did not vanish. Among the Abenakis of St. Francis, this role was filled by the "Prayer Chief", in whom we can certainly see a vestige of the old office of dogique:

One of the great chiefs was named "Chief of the Prayer". This chief was the first in the church, after the missionary; he presided over the prayers which were made in common in the church each day, he took care that each person was exact to fulfill his religious obligations, he reprimanded the wicked and the negligent, and did not leave them rest until they presented themselves to the missionary. (Maurault 1866:567, translation mine)

Confraternity of the Holy Family and of the Servitude of the Blessed Virgin

The Confraternity of the Holy Family was not strictly an community founded by natives, but it figures very prominently in the missions. A very important chapter was founded among the most devout Iroquois at St. Francis Xavier du Sault, shaping the spiritual lives of some of the greatest lights of that mission.

The branch of the confraternity for lay women and girls came about at the initiative of the Madame Barbe d'Ailleboust (d. 1685), with the consultation of Fr. Chaumonot. D'Ailleboust was the widow of the governor of New France, and her skill in the Algonquin language was such that she was able to teach it to Sulpician missionaries. The association was founded in July 31, 1673 in Montreal; it spread from there throughout Canada and exists to this day.

Father Pierron introduced the confraternity to La Prairie, and Catherine Gandeaktena was instrumental in promoting it there. The *Jesuit Relation* of 1672–1673 is effusive in attributing great spiritual graces to this association:

> It is rare to see a really devout man who is not a true servant of Our Lady. For that reason, a confraternity of the Holy Family and of the Servitude of the Blessed Virgin has been established in this Mission. It is an assembly composed of our most fervent Christians. They meet together every Sunday to ascertain whether all the rules are observed, and to learn what good can be done and what evil prevented. It would take too long to describe in detail all the devotions of this holy confraternity, and to relate their tender devotion to Our Lady, their charity toward their neighbors, their zeal for the salvation of their countrymen. I shall content myself with saying that all the good in this Mission comes from this abundant source of all kinds of blessings. In fact, it is the members of this association who attract the

81

Iroquois hither, who instruct them, who prepare them for baptism. It is they also who preserve and maintain the fervor of the new Christians, and who thus prepare them to reign one day in heaven (JR 58:87).

Mohawk Prayers for the confraternity are given in the *Book of Seven Nations*, and the chaplet specific to its members has already been described earlier (see page 64).

Kateri's Band

> You will be pleased to hear from me respecting the austerities practiced by certain savage women...religious life began to please them very much, and three of them formed an association, in order to commence a sort of Convent; but we stopped them, because we did not think that the time had yet come for this. However, even if they were not cloistered, they at least observed Chastity; and one of them died with the reputation of sanctity, 3 years ago next spring. They, and some others who imitated them, would be admired in France, if what they do were known there.
>
> —Fr. Claude Chauchetiere (JR 64:175)

Blessed Kateri Tekakwitha and her two closest friends Marie-Thérèse Tegaiaguenta, an Oneida, and Marie Skarichions, a Huron of Lorette, conceived of the idea of starting a convent together on Heron Island in the St. Lawrence. However, their inexperience with formal religious life and the dangers of the location they chose caused their priest to refuse consent to this venture.

Obediently, the three holy women accepted his judgment and continued on as an informal pious association—with no less fervor:

> The sort of monastery that they maintain here has its rules. They have promised God never to put on their gala-dress (for the savage women have some taste, and

take pride in adorning themselves with porcelain beads; with vermilion, which they apply to their Cheeks; and with earrings and bracelets). They assist One another in the fields; They meet together to incite one another to virtue; and one of them has been received as a nun in The hospital of monreal. (JR 64:179)

An in-depth analysis of the spirituality of Kateri's band is outside the scope of the present study, but some of its main aspects included a vow of perpetual virginity, communal work, and a heavy emphasis on mortification of the flesh. Of this last practice in particular, it should be noted that Kateri bade her friend Marie-Therese to never give it up.

Chauchetiere's biography gives us Kateri's daily rule of life as given to her by her confessor: rising at 4 AM to go the chapel, attending two Masses and receiving Communion whenever possible, making frequent visits to the Blessed Sacrament, going to Confession every week, and making spiritual communions throughout the day (*Positio*:175).

We know of the Saturday devotions performed by Kateri and Marie-Therese:

> every Saturday, the two friends prepared their confessions in a more out-of-the-way place, a plank cabin in the middle of the cemetery. There they devoutly recited their Act of contrition or some other prayer that appealed to them, always ending with an act of faith. Despite Marie-Therese's objections, Kateri, wishing to be the first to do penance, fell on her knees. Marie-Therese was strong-armed, and the third blow drew blood; still Kateri always complained that her friend did not strike hard enough. After a first series of such blows, they had the habit of saying the Holy Family Rosary. This prayer they interrupted many times; at each interruption, they gave themselves five strokes. (Bechard 1976:170)

Portrait of Kateri Tekakwitha by Fr. Claude Chauchetiere, now kept at the church of St. Francis Xavier in Kahnawake. Made between 1682–1693.

Kateri adopted a simple style of dress which could well be viewed as an Iroquois-style habit. Chauchetiere tells us that the young women of the Sault were accustomed to give proper attention to hairstyles, fine clothes, and jewelry, but that Kateri herself renounced red blankets and ornaments and wore only a simple new blue blanket for the days she received Holy Communion.

This blue blanket is shown covering Kateri's head as a veil in Chauchetiere's portrait (see previous page). She wore it thus even outdoors, as much for the modesty it afforded her as well as to give a respite for her sensitive eyesight. Other women of the mission, Cholenec tells us, normally wore the blanket on the shoulders. In church functions they then brought it over the head as a chapel veil, as seen in Chauchetiere's sketch captioned "The faithful take part in the processions of the Blessed Sacrament." Engravings 200 years later still showed Kahnawake women with these same kinds of blanket-veils before the Blessed Sacrament at Corpus Christi (Bechard 1976, following page 74; L'Opinion Publique 1870).

Kateri's dress appears have been adopted by the rest of her band. Marie Skarichions had seen nuns at Montreal and it was apparently her idea that the community dress alike. Chauchetiere's quote above notes the women's vow to never "put on their gala-dress." Perhaps they regularly wore veils as well: his sketch captioned "The first chapel is building" shows three veiled women—outdoors and in a context quite outside of liturgical functions—sitting at the foot of a cross and looking out over the St. Lawrence River while construction is going on at the chapel. These figures almost certainly represent Kateri, Marie-Therese, and Marie imagining their monastery on Heron Island (Bechard 1976, following page 74).

There is contemporary notice of Kateri's band as still existing in the early 1690s (Positio:332; JR 64:125). However, the subsequent history of the group is unknown.

+ Concluding Remarks +

The only true, authentic inculturators are not theologians, or bishops, but the saints.
                        —Archbishop Chaput (Buckenmeyer 2007)

The last 40 years have seen a great deal of attention paid to the concept of inculturation—and it has often been simply taken for granted that current liturgical styles, which draw from that concept, have given us a more complete fusion of Catholic practice and native culture than anything seen in the period before Vatican II. Yet it would be well to consider whether this is indeed the case.

It may be true that today's inculturated liturgies *look* more Indian than the Indian Masses described in this book. Old photographs of pre-Vatican II American Indian priests such as Abbé Prosper Vincent, Fr. Michael Jacobs, or Fr. James Chrysostom Bouchard do not show obviously Indian features, and neither do the mission churches themselves. The modern liturgies depicted on the Tekakwitha Conference website, however, feature a striking array of obvious Indian symbols and styles. Native cloths and artistic styles are well represented, a great deal of attention is given to native clothing styles, native dances are inserted into the liturgy, and prayer implements such as pipes, cedar branches, feathers, and smudge sticks figure prominently.

Yet these additions represent only a small and rather superficial subset of preselected American Indian customs. It is clear that too arbitrary a line has been drawn around what is authentic matter for inculturation when, for example, certain novel practices like liturgical dance—which was never practiced by American Indian

Catholics before Vatican II—are aggressively promoted at the expense of ones that have a long and well-documented history among American Indian Catholics, such as native plainchant and the *pain benit*. If inculturation truly purports to give a whole and complete expression of native culture in the Church, it cannot afford to limit itself to the experiments of post-Vatican II liturgical progressivism. It must include, and even give prominence to, the traditions that American Indian Catholicism has painstakingly built over the last 300 years.

Pope Benedict XVI, in his work *Spirit of the Liturgy* published prior to his elevation, has cited both superficiality and experimentalism as some of the major problems with inculturation today:

> Everywhere these days the liturgy seems to be the proving ground for experiments in inculturation. Whenever people talk about inculturation, they almost always think only of the liturgy, which then has to undergo often quite dismal distortions. The worshippers usually groan at this, though it is happening for their sake. An inculturation that is more or less just an alteration of outward forms is not inculturation at all, but a misunderstanding of inculturation. Moreover, it frequently insults cultural and religious communities, from whom liturgical forms are borrowed in an all too superficial and external way. (Ratzinger 2000:200–201)

Rather than experimentation with imagery and stereotypic tropes, Ratzinger envisioned a deeper and more natural exchange of cultural gifts in the depths of popular piety, which he called "the soil without which the liturgy cannot thrive." Decrying the tendency of some liturgists to dismiss or abuse popular piety, he sets forth the process by which nurturing it can naturally and effortlessly give rise to ritual traditions:

Corpus Christi procession at St. Francis Xavier, Kahnawake. From l'Opinon Publique (1870).

Instead one must love it [popular piety], purifying and
guiding it where necessary, but always accepting it with
great reverence, even when it seems alien or alienating,
as the dedicated sanctuary of faith in the hearts of the
people. It is faith's secure inner rooting; when it dries
up, rationalism and sectarianism have an easy job.
Tried and tested elements of popular piety may pass
over, then, into liturgical celebration, without officious
or hasty fabrication, by a patient process of lengthy
growth. (ibid:202)

As this book has tried to show, exactly such a natural and
spontaneous process had been unfolding in the Indian missions
from the colonial age to just before the Vatican Council.

In the hearts of generations of Christian Indians over the
centuries, a holistic fusion of culture and religion had taken place.
Popular piety moved them to translate and learn the chants of the
Church, produce devotional wampum, and keep such customs alive
as the pax board and the *pain benit* when these were going extinct in
the Anglo-American and French Canadian parishes around them.
And it was popular piety also—and here some past mistakes have
to be frankly admitted—that led many native Catholics to feel such
intense discomfort when the traditional Indian Mass was abruptly
discontinued and a wholly unfamiliar English liturgy was put in its
place.

Nonetheless, while it is true that the last 40 years represent
a rather sharp break in the development of the American Indian
liturgies, to simply abolish their memory and proceed as if they
themselves never happened would require an equally jarring
discontinuity. No congregation wants to be tossed about from
one pole to another as successive pastors impose radically different
visions of liturgical perfection—that would be repugnant to the
sense of the faithful who expect stability in liturgical forms. Change
is certainly allowable and perhaps sometimes even required, yet
not by cycles of revolution and restoration but by a process of
organic growth and maturation. This process is one of centuries,

not years, as successive generations work to distill the best of what their ancestors had to offer and work also to filter out of liturgical practice what is merely trendy from what is timeless.

Simply put, inculturation at its core must give priority to the preservation of tradition, so that the fruits of past generations can be put to use in the continued dialogue between culture and religion. Certainly it cannot be said that every single one of the customs of previous days—even those of long usage in the Indian missions—are sacrosanct in their own right and must by divine mandate be preserved in perpetuity. Yet they all call for a certain respect by the very fact that they were shaped and molded by ten generations of American Indian Catholics: from the first converts of the colonial era to the very dawn of the Space Age, from the Huron captives of the Iroquois Wars to the high-steel Mohawks who built the skyscrapers of Manhattan.

The objection could perhaps be raised that the pre-Vatican II period is simply not relevant to today's Catholicism, and that the historical Church and its liturgy are really European developments which are not suitable to the spiritual needs of indigenous Americans. There may well be some who believe that Catholicism needs to be freed entirely from its Old World shackles and re-dressed into an indigenous form by clothing it entirely in Native American culture.

But the Church is not and never has been a purely European entity. True, that our historical education in the West most associates Catholicism with medieval European culture, and perhaps understandably, given the way Latin Christianity had become so intertwined with European life since the fall of Rome. Yet a wider historical and geographical view of the Church serves as a strong corrective against such continental narrowness. Of the five great Patriarchates of Christianity, two were in Asia (Antioch and Jerusalem) and one in Africa (Alexandria). Moreover, the Patriarchate of Byzantium, though technically located on the European side of the Bosporus, was historically so affected by

Near-Eastern spirituality and thought that it, too, has always been classified as an Eastern Church.

From the Syrians of Antioch and the Copts of Egypt, a faith that never once touched European soil radiated out to regions that were barely even known to Latin Christians before the Age of Exploration. In the 4th century, the patriarch of Alexandria commissioned St. Frumentius to evangelize Ethiopia, giving rise to a distinctive Ethiopian Christianity older than that of many countries in Europe. Syrian missionaries forged west into the heart of Asia, giving rise to Chaldean Christianity in modern Iraq. On the southwestern coast of India were the Syro-Malabar Christians, traditionally founded from St. Thomas the Apostle. In the 7th century, Christianity was even planted in China, a fact of which we have invaluable testimony from the inscription of Xi'an.

These Christian communities remained largely outside the development of Latin Christianity for centuries—so they give us an excellent idea of what Apostolic Christianity looks like outside of the culture of Western Europe. And, truth be told, it does not bear a close resemblance to the liturgical experiments of the last 40 years. To cite but one example, the post-Vatican II period has seen a rather aggressive removal of pious devotions and adornments—but if anything, the exuberance of the Asian and African Churches makes medieval Latin Christianity look stark and restrained by comparison.

A historical study of Western Christianity itself is also instructive in establishing how the religion and the culture interact to form a ritual tradition. Catholicism came to be what it is in Europe not so much because either Hebrew Christianity was de-Judaized or Hellenic Christianity was de-Hellenized for the use of Romans, but because pagan Roman culture, influenced by Greek thought and influenced by Hebrew Scriptures, was gradually transformed by the sanctifying power of the Church within it. The inculturation of Gentile nations, in other words, came about not so much because the Church conformed to the culture but because the culture conformed to the Church.

Specific, planned adaptation in the liturgy can and does happen, as is proved by the heroic efforts of Sts. Cyril and Methodius among the Slavs. But it is worth noting that neither those saints nor their Slavic converts repudiated the Byzantine tradition in the process; rather, they remained solidly within it and enriched it with, among other things, a new ecclesiastical language called Old Church Slavonic. Likewise, the Ethiopians and the Syro-Malabarese hold as tenaciously to their respective Coptic and Syriac heritage as to their own local traditions. And as we have seen in the case of St. Francis Xavier du Sault and elsewhere, it was quite often American Indians themselves who took the initiative to learn the liturgies and chants of the Roman Church. History, then, very much argues against any idea that inculturation gives a license for de-Romanizing American Indian Christianity. Rather, it suggests that the Roman Rite forms a solid Apostolic base that can then be enriched—not replaced—by local cultural expression.

Inculturation which excludes established native tradition finds itself necessarily reinventing the wheel. It is easy to see, for example, that the reason smudging was not introduced sooner in the missions is that the Indian Mass already had something very like it. Only when the liturgy was totally stripped of its clouds of incense did smudging have to come into being to fill the void. Four-directional prayer is also seen as an important advance of inculturation, yet before the priest turned his back to the tabernacle and toward the people in what Benedict XVI has called "a self-enclosed circle," the Indian Mass had priest and congregation both face east to the rising sun—the altar forming an epicenter around which the whole world was oriented: the Gospel was proclaimed to liturgical north, the Epistle liturgical south, and the congregation stood in expectant waiting from the liturgical west.

It would seem harder, if not impossible, to make that same case for something like liturgical dance. But the Indian Mass was itself far more a dance than the modern liturgy, which expects very little sacred movement from its participants. In former days, it was not just a few select individuals enacting a dance at a certain time, but everyone—priests, deacons, acolytes and members of the congregation—throughout the entire liturgy all fulfilling their appointed roles in orchestrating a complex sequence of genuflections, bows, signs of the cross, and processions. True liturgical dance was and is not merely a dance *in* the liturgy, but the dance *of* the liturgy.

Before offering some suggestions on how such a historically inclusive view impacts the future of inculturation, I want to first admit that a layman such as myself cannot presume to fashion a pastoral plan for mission communities I have never even set foot in just because I have buried my nose in historical documents. There has been too much of such armchair liturgical sermonizing of late. And to what extent native—or any communities for that matter—will retain the new Missal or restore the use of the Missal of Blessed John XXIII, now freed again for use throughout the Church, is a matter best left to the parishes themselves and their pastors and bishops—with, we pray, all their attention to the good of souls.

Having said so, it should be emphatically stated that we would do ourselves a disservice to view the ritual traditions in this book—even if they are currently not practiced—as purely historical museum pieces. Many of them, and probably even all of them, could well be given a new lease on life in the years to come.

Private devotions are easy enough to revive with a simple act of the will. Public liturgical restorations, of course, require more in the way of permissions and participation from pastors and bishops. But as nothing has been described here save for the traditions that historically existed in the missions, and as these traditions flourished under a climate that—it must be admitted for good or ill—was far less permissive than that of today, there is every reason to be confident that they can be restored to their full glory and continue in their organic development that was so unnaturally truncated in the late 1960s.

Benedict XVI's recent motu proprio *Summorum Pontificum* has at last restored the use of the ancient Roman liturgy to the Latin church, so the way is now open for a full revival of the Indian Masses as part of the Church's daily life. And many aspects of the traditional Indian Masses can quite easily be applied to the new liturgy as well. Native-language Propers and hymns can easily be worked into a choir's repertoire. And the continuity with the pre-conciliar period could be even more complete if the Propers and hymns chosen for the Mass were not left to the whims of choir directors but followed as closely as possible the cycles that were already in existence before the Council, of which we have evidence in such books as the *Book of Seven Nations* and the *Kaiatonsera Teieriwakwatha*.

There does not seem to be any reason why the old Indian Mass cannot have a suitable equivalent in the *Novus Ordo Missae*: with the priest's portion of the liturgy in English and with Propers and ordinaries in Mohawk, Micmac, Ojibwe, or whatever language is traditional to the particular mission. By doing so, and wholly in the spirit of *Summorum Pontificum*, there could be not one but two forms of the Indian Mass going forward—both grounded in the Roman liturgy but both also sharing in a common 300-year-old American Indian tradition as well.

One thing that is indispensable to any efforts of revival and reform is more exhaustive research in the mission archives. Scholars trained in American linguistics and in the Roman liturgy—who have become decidedly less common than they used to be—must delve deeply into the manuscript and published works, analyze them, and make the information they gain available to a non-specialist audience. Of course, if any liturgical changes result from such research, they should not be foisted on the people but should be prudently introduced, perhaps optionally at first, with every respect for the forms that are already in place at the missions and which parishioners have long been accustomed to.

One happy side effect of the revival of the Indian Mass, and one which needs to be taken more seriously by linguists and anthropologists, would be its singular advantage as a preserver of language and culture. Native languages, most of which are now under some threat of extinction, can find the Church an indispensible aid to their preservation and continued use. American Indian Catholics may not be able to hear their ancestral languages on the streets or in their homes, but Sunday after Sunday they could hear them fill the vaults of the churches. If liturgy can preserve Hebrew, Latin, and Coptic for thousands of years without any native speakers, it could certainly do the same for Mohawk and Algonquin as well. Language preservation, in turn, allows the revival of the great art forms of native hymnody, chant, and polyphony, and skilled composers can continue to expand the repertoire. A whole body of existing native-language sermons, rites, and devotional texts could then be translated and published for the benefit of a wider audience beyond the limits of reservations to America and the halls of Rome itself, as the particular genius of American Indian spirituality is disposed for the benefit of the universal Church.

The Church can further serve as a patron of American Indian arts, as it has served European art for over a thousand years. Native textile work can be commissioned for sacred use, and it is not hard to imagine native women trained in their own traditional styles of beadwork producing beautiful chasubles, altar cloths, copes, and all the necessary adornments that surround the Divine Liturgy. The fashioning of wampum belts is another custom easily revived—and it can be not only an occasion to preserve a centuries-old art form but also a means of prayerful devotion, analogous to the icon-writers of the East.

And what is there to now prevent native religious communities from finally realizing the dream that Blessed Kateri, Marie, and Marie Therese once had gazing at Heron Island from the banks of the St. Lawrence River? Communities of native nuns could well continue in the spirit of the prototypic Katerian rule forged three centuries ago, perhaps even taking as a sacred habit the traditional Kahnawake vestments and veil seen in Chauchetiere's portrait of

Blessed Kateri—in much the same way as another American saint, St. Elizabeth Ann Seton, in her day adapted the widow's weeds. Societies of devout priests could also arise, rigorously trained in native spirituality, in language, and especially in the preservation of native liturgies and devotions—so that the sacraments are never absent from mission churches again. We dare even hope that someday some monasteries and seminaries would form, esteemed as much for their piety as for their learning, which are specifically dedicated to preserving, teaching, and living the very traditions described in this book.

It is, of course, God's will to determine to what degree these things will ever come about. Visions of idyllic Indian Catholic communities have danced before the eyes of pious men and women from the earliest missionaries to Fr. Pierre-Jean DeSmet. And even these saintly individuals soon found that history teaches us fierce lessons about seeking Paradise in this world rather than the next one. But it is also true that all things come to pass in their due time, and it is not our place to prejudge the Divine Will when that time is. Perhaps, just past the turn of the third millennium, there is no better moment for us to more fully integrate the whole of Indian Catholic history from the 1600s to the present and to prudently consider the best ways to meld the gifts of that cultural legacy to the mission of the Church. In so doing, we would be paying our due respect to the past generations who faithfully preserved the traditions described in this book and to the future generations who expect us to hand it to them intact.

APPENDICES

Appendix A: Mass of Trinity Sunday according to the Use of Akwesasne

The Mass given here has been collated from two sources. The Mohawk ordinaries and Propers have been taken directly from the Mass Asenseratokenti (Holy Trinity) of the Kaiatonsera Teieriwakwatha. There are some obvious typographical errors in the Mohawk, but as I am unqualified to correct these I have kept to what is given in the book.

The Latin text, including the spoken Propers (Collect, Secret, Postcommunion) is taken from the Missal of 1962, which is the currently approved form of the traditional Mass according to the motu proprio Summorum Pontificum. In keeping with the standard practice on Trinity Sunday, I have included the second Propers for the commemoration of the first Sunday after Pentecost, including the changed Last Gospel; without the commemoration this would normally be from the first chapter of John.

ASPERGES

Asknekoserawe, Sewenniio ohnekatokenti nok akiatakenratane. Askiatohare nok enkenni oniete.

Sewenniio takitenr nisa tsini akwa satanitenraskon kowa

V. Ahonwasenaiien Roniha nok Roienha nok Rotkon Roiatatokenti.
R. Tsini iohtonne tsinahe ethonaiohtonhake nonwa, tiotkon oni tsinenwe ethonaiawen.

Asknekoserawe, Sewenniio ohnekatokenti nok akiatakenratane. Askiatohare nok enkenni oniete.

Ostende nobis, Domine, misericordiam tuam.
R. *Et salutare tuum da nobis.*
P. Domine, exaudi orationem meam.
R. *Et clamor meus ad te veniat.*
P. Dominus vobiscum.
R. *Et cum spiritu tuo.*
P. Oremus.

Exaudi nos, Domine sancte, Pater omnipotens, aeterne Deus, et mittere digneris sanctum Angelum tuum de caelis, qui custodiat, foveat, protegat, visitet, atque defendat omnes habitantes in hoc habitaculo. Per Christum Dominum nostrum.

R. *Amen.*

MASS OF THE CATECHUMENS

IONTAWEIATAKWATHA (INTROIT)

Atsitewasennaien Asenseratokenti shaiatat ok ne Niio
Rawenniio, hetsitewanentonnion, aseken sonkwentenron ne
nonwentsiakwekon tsionkwe. Niio Sewenniio tsi iakionnhe,
akwa ionehrakwat tsini tsennanoron nonwensiakwekon.
Ahonwasenaiien Roniha nok Roienha nok Rotkon Roiatatokenti.
Tsini iohtonne tsinahe ethonaiohtonhake nonwa, tiotkon oni
tsinenwe ethonaiawen.

PRAYERS AT THE FOOT OF THE ALTAR

In nomine Patris, + et Filii, et Spiritus Sancti. Amen.
P. Introibo ad altare Dei.
R. *Ad Deum qui laetificat juventutem meam.*
P. Judica me, Deus et discerne causam meam de gente non sanct:
ab homine iniquo, et doloso erue me.
R. *Quia tu es, Deus, fortitudo mea: quare me repulisti; et quare tristis
incedo, dum affligit me inimicus?*
P. Emitte lucem tuam, et veritatem tuam: ipsa me deduxerunt, et
adduxerunt in montem sanctum tuum et in tabernacula tua.
R. *Et introibo ad altare Dei, ad Deum qui laetificat juventutem meam.*
P. Confitebor tibi in cithara, Deus, Deus meus: quare tristis es,
anima mea, et quare conturbas me?
R. *Spera in Deo, quoniam adhuc confitebor illi: salutare vultus mei, et
Deus meus.*
P. Gloria Patri, et Filio, et Spiritui Sancto.
R. *Sicut erat in principio, et nunc, et semper, et in saecula saeculorum.
Amen.*
P. Introibo ad altare Dei.
R. *Ad Deum qui laetificat juventutem meam.*
P. Adjutorium nostrum + in nomine Domini.

R. *Qui fecit caelum et terram.*

P. Confiteor Deo omnipotenti, beatae Mariae semper Virgini, beato Michaeli archangelo, beato Joanni Baptistae, sanctis Apostolis Petro et Paulo, omnibus Sanctis, et vobis, fratres, quia peccavi nimis cogitatione, verbo et opere: mea culpa, mea culpa, mea maxima culpa. Ideo precor beatam Mariam semper Virginem, beatum Michaelem Archangelum, beatum Joannem Baptistam, sanctos Apostolos Petrum et Paulum, omnes Sanctos, et vos, fratres, orare pro me ad Dominum Deum nostrum.

R: *Misereatur tui omnipotens Deus, et, dimissis peccatis tuis, perducat te ad vitam aeternam.*

P. Amen.

R. *Confiteor Deo omnipotenti, beatae Mariae semper Virgini, beato Michaeli archangelo, beato Joanni Baptistae, sanctis Apostolis Petro et Paulo, omnibus Sanctis, et tibi, Pater, quia peccavi nimis cogitatione, verbo et opere: mea culpa, mea culpa, mea maxima culpa . Ideo precor beatam Mariam semper Virginem, beatum Michaelem Archangelum, beatum Joannem Baptistam, sanctos Apostolos Petrum et Paulum, omnes Sanctos, et te, Pater, orare pro me ad Dominum Deum nostrum.*

P: Misereatur vestri omnipotens Deus, et dimissis peccatis vestris, perducat vos ad vitam aeternam.

R. *Amen.*

P. Indulgentiam, + absolutionem et remissionem peccatorum nostrorum tribuat nobis omnipotens et misericors Dominus.

R. *Amen.*

P. Deus, tu conversus vivificabis nos.

R. *Et plebs tua laetabitur in te.*

P. Ostende nobis, Domine, misericordiam tuam.

R. *Et salutare tuum da nobis.*

P. Domine, exaudi orationem meam.

R. *Et clamor meus ad te veniat.*

P. Dominus vobiscum.

R. *Et cum spiritu tuo.*

P. Oremus.

Aufer a nobis, quaesumus Domine, iniquitates nostras: ut ad sancta Sanctorum puris mereamur mentibus introire. Per Christum Dominum nostrum. Amen.

Oramus te, Domine, per merita Sanctorum tuorum, quorum reliquiae hic sunt, et omnium Sanctorum, ut indulgere digneris omnia peccata mea. Amen.

KYRIE ELEISON

P. Takwentenr Sewenniio.
R. *Takwentenr Sewenniio.*
P. Takwentenr Sewenniio.
R. *Kristos takwentenr.*
P. Kristos takwentenr.
R. *Kristos takwentenr.*
P. Takwentenr Sewenniio.
R. *Takwentenr Sewenniio.*
P. Takwentenr Sewenniio.

GLORIA IN EXCELSIS

Gloria in Excelsis Deo. Nok nonwentsiake skennen kenhak nonkwe iakonikonhriio. Tekwanonweratons. Kwatsennonniase. Kwasennaiens. Kwaronhiaientons. Kwatonraseronse tsini akwa saiatanehrakwat. Sewenniio iesennakeraton Niio iahte sanoronse. Sewenniio sonha Hiaienha Niio Iesos Kristos. Sewenniio hetsenikonhraiewenthos Hianiha Niio. Seriwahtontha kariwaneren katakwentenr nisa. Seriwahtontha kariwaneren satontat onen nonwa ne kwennitha. Ne satiens tsi raweientehtakon Hianiha katakwentenr nisa. Aseken sonha saiatatokenti. Sonha Sewenniio. Sonha tsiatanoron Iesos Kristos. Rotkon Roiatatokenti Niio Roniha ietsisennaiens. Etho naiawen.

P. Dominus vobiscum.
R. *Et cum spiritu tuo.*

COLLECT

P. Oremus.
Omnipotens sempiterne Deus, qui dedisti famulis tuis in confessione verae fidei, aeternae Trinitatis gloriam agnoscere, et in potentia majestatis adorare Unitatem: quaesumus; ut ejusdem fidei firmitate, ab omnibus semper muniamur adversis. Per Dominum.

COLLECT (Commemoration of the Sunday)

P. Oremus.
Deus, in te sperantium fortitudo, adesto propitius invocationibus nostris: et quia sine te nihil potest mortalis infirmitas, praesta auxilium gratiae tuae; ut in exsequendis mandatis tuis, et voluntate tibi et actione placeamus. Per Dominum.
R. Amen.

EPISTLE

Lectio Epistolæ beati Pauli Apostoli ad Romanos.
O Altitudo divitiarum sapientiae, et scientiae Dei: quam incomprehensibilia sunt judicia ejus, et investigabiles viae ejus! Quis enim cognovit sensum Domini? Aut quis consiliarius ejus fuit? Aut quis prior dedit illi, et retribuetur ei? Quoniam ex ipso, et per ipsum, et in ipso sunt omnia: ipsi gloria in saecula. Amen.
R. Deo Gratias.

ARERIIA (ALLELUIA)

Areriia, areriia. Sonha tsiatanoron, Niio Sewenniio takwaiatison, iesasennaien iahte kakont.

TEHNIRONHIAKEHRONON

Tehnironhiakehronon tehniriwakwakwe hiatontakwe.
Saiatatokenti, Saiatatokenti, Saiatatokenti,
    Sewenniio Niio Sabaoth:
Iaonwentsiananon onwentsiakwekon saiatanehrakwatsera.
Asen nihati raonhakon Niio karonhiake Roniha, Roienha nok
Rotkon Roiatatokenti, ashen nihati, shaiatat ok Niio.
Saiatatokenti, Saiatatokenti, Saiatatokenti,
    Sewenniio Niio Sabaoth:
Ahonwasennaien Roniha nok Roienha nok Rotkon Roiatatokenti,
ashen nihati, shaiatat ok Niio.
Iaonwentsiananon onwentsiakwekon saiatanehrakwatsera.

Munda cor meum ac labia mea, omnipotens Deus, qui labia
Isaiae prophetae calculo mundasti ignito: ita me tua grata
miseratione dignare mundare, ut sanctum Evangelium tuum,
digne valeam nuntiare. Per Christum Dominum nostrum. Amen.
Jube Domine benedicere. Dominus sit in corde meo et in labiis
meis: ut digne et competenter annuntiem Evangelium suum: In
nomine Patris, et Filii, + et Spiritus Sancti. Amen.

P. Dominus vobiscum.
R. *Et cum spiritu tuo.*

GOSPEL

P. Sequentia sancti Evangelii secundum Matthaeum.
R. *Gloria tibi, Domine.*
In illo tempore: Dixit Jesus discipulis suis: Data est mihi omnis
potestatis in caelo, et in terra. Euntes ergo docete omnes gentes,
baptizantes eos in nomine Patris, et Filii, et Spiritus Sancti:
docentes eos servare omnia quaecumque mandavi vobis. Et ecce
ego vobiscum sum omnibus diebus, usque ad consummationem
saeculi.

R. *Laus tibi, Christe.*
P. Per evangelica dicta deleantur nostra delicta.

HOMILY

(Here the Homily may be given)

NICENE CREED

Credo in Unum Deum. Roniha iahte honoronse roson karonhia
nonwentsia. Akewekon tsini iekens nok tsini iahte iekens.
Nok saiatat Rawenniio Iesos Kristos raonha Niio Roienha.
Ok tsi hiatatienha tsinahe iahte kakonte. Teioswatetakwa
teioswatetakwake akwa Niio raonhake Niio. Roienha iahte
honwason sahniiatat Roniha Akwekon roteweiennison. Ii
tionkwe sonkwaniente sonkwatsennonniatennire karonhiake
thawenonton. Raonniaton raieronke Rotkon Roiatatokenti
aonekwensa Wari iahte kanakwaienteri nok onkwe rotonhon, nok
onkwe, onkwe rotonhon. Onkwariwa ronwaiatanentakton Pilat
roterihontakwe rawenheion ronwaiataten. Nok shotonnheton
asen watontha tsini kahiatonkwe. Karonhiake shawenonton tsi
raweientehtakon Roniha. Sekon tentre enthonehrekwatonhatie
tensakoiatoret iakonnhe nok iakowentahon, tiotkon, tiotkon
enhonwennakeratse. Nok Rotkon Roiatatokenti Rawenniio
sonkionnheton rononhake Roniha Roienhathoientakon.
Ne Roniha nok Roienha satehonwatiwenniiostha
satehonwatisennaiens Rotitokensehakwe ronwatrori. Enskat
ok Kentiohkwatokenti Ratikwekonne tehonarenihon.
tehonarenihon. Twakehtakon enskat iontatenekwahestha
swaterakewatha kariwaneren. Wakerhare tsinentsiontonnhete
iakowentahon. Nok iahte kakont entsiakonnheke. Etho naiawen.

MASS OF THE FAITHFUL

P. Dominus vobiscum.

R. *Et cum spiritu tuo.*

P. Oremus.

ISE SASHENSERATOKENTI

Ise Sashenseratokenti, Saiatanehrakwat, ashen nitsion, Sesiatat ok Niio Tiotkon senakere, Nok iahte kakonte ensenakereke.

Ise Sashenseratokenti, Tiesariwakwase Orhonkehne nok iekarahane Iakoriwiioston Ne nonwentsiakwekon Ne tienakerenion.

Ise Sashenseratokenti, Tiesatontsothase, Iesennitha, iesawenniiostha, Tsini tsiatanoron, Ne iakorharenion, Ne nashetenranion.

Ise Sashenseratokenti, Eronhiakehronon Iesanentons tiotkon ne rontonnions: Saiatatokenti, Saiatatokenti, Saiatatokenti.

Ise Sashenseratokenti, Sesiatat ok Niio, Iesaniha nok Iesaienha, Ise oni Satkon Saiatatokenti, Tekwanonweratons.

OFFERTORY PRAYERS

Suscipe, sancte Pater, omnipotens aeterne Deus, hanc immaculatem Hostiam, quam ego indignus famulus tuus offero tibi, Deo meo vivo et vero, pro innumerabilibus peccatis, et offensionibus, et negligentiis meis, et pro omnibus circumstantibus; sed et pro omnibus fidelibus Christianis, vivis atque defunctis: ut mihi et illis proficiat ad salutem in vitam aeternam. Amen.

Deus, + qui humanae substantiae dignitatem mirabiliter condidisti, et mirabilius reformasti: da nobis per hujus aquae et vini mysterium, ejus divinitatis esse consortes, qui humanitatis nostrae fieri dignatus est particeps, Jesus Christus, Filius tuus, Dominus noster: qui tecum vivit et regnat in unitate Spiritus Sancti Deus, per omnia saecula saeculorum. Amen.

Offerimus tibi, Domine, calicem salutaris, tuam deprecantes clementiam, ut in conspectu divinae majestatis tuae, pro nostra et totius mundi salute cum odore suavitatis ascendat. Amen.

In spiritu humilitatis et in animo contrito suscipiamur a te, Domine: et sic fiat sacrificium nostrum in conspectu tuo hodie, ut placeat tibi, Domine Deus.

Veni, Sanctificator omnipotens, aeterne Deus: et bene+dic hoc sacrificium, tuo sancto nomini praeparatum.

Per intercessionem beati Michaelis Archangeli, stantis a dextris altaris incensi, et omnium electorum suorum, incensum istud dignetur Dominus bene+dicere, et in odorem suavitatis accipere. Per Christum Dominum nostrum. Amen.

Incensum istud a te benedictum, ascendat ad te, Domine: et descendat super nos misericordia tua.

Dirigatur, Domine, oratio mea, sicut incensum, in conspectu tuo: elevatio manuum mearum sacrificium vespertinum. Pone, Domine, custodiam ori meo, et ostium circumstantiae labiis meis: ut non declinet cor meum in verba malitiae, ad excusandas excusationes in peccatis.

Accendat in nobis Dominus ignem sui amoris, et flammam aeternae caritatis. Amen.

Lavabo inter innocentes manus meas: et circumdabo altare tuum, Domine.
Ut audiam vocem laudis: et enarrem universa mirabilia tua.

Domine, dilexi decorem domus tuae: et locum habitationis gloriae tuaae.
Ne perdas cum impiis, Deus, animam meam, et cum viris sanguinum vitam meam.
In quorum manibus iniquitates sunt: dextera eorum repleta est muneribus.
Ego autem in innocentia mea ingressus sum: redime me, et miserere mei.
Pes meus stetit in directo: in ecclesiis benedicam te, Domine.

Gloria Patri, et Filio, et Spiritui Sancto. Sicut erat in principio, et nunc, et semper: et in saecula saeculorum.
Amen

Suscipe, sancta Trinitas, hanc oblationem, quam tibi offerimus ob memoriam passionis, resurrectionis et ascensionis Jesu Christi Domini nostri: et in honorem beatae Mariae semper Virginis, et beati Joannis Baptistae, et sanctorum Apostolorum Petri et Pauli, et istorum et omnium Sanctorum: ut illis proficiat ad honorem, nobis autem ad salutem: et illi pro nobis intercedere dignentur in caelis, quorum memoriam agimus in terris. Per eumdem Christum Dominum nostrum. Amen.

Orate, fratres, ut meum ac vestrum sacrificium acceptabile fiat apud Deum Patrem omnipotentem.
R. Suscipiat Dominus sacrificium de manibus tuis, ad laudem et gloriam nominis sui, ad utilitatem quoque nostram, totiusque Ecclesiae suae sanctae.

SECRET

Sanctifica, quaesumus Domine Deus noster, per tui sancti nominis invocationem, hujus oblationis hostiam: et per eam nosmetipsos tibi perfice munus aeternum. Per Dominum.

SECRET (Commemoration of the Sunday)

Hostias nostras, quaesumus, Domine, tibi dicatas placatus assume; et, ad perpetuum nobis tribue provenire subsidium. Per Dominum.
R. Amen.

PREFACE

P. Dominus vobiscum.
R. Et cum spiritu tuo.
P. Sursum corda.
R. Habemus ad Dominum.
P. Gratias agamus Domino Deo nostro.
R. Dignum et justum est.

Vere dignum et justum est, aequum et salutare, nos tibi semper, et ubique gratias agere: Domine sancte, Pater omnipotens, aeterne Deus: Qui cum Unigenito Filio tuo, et Spiritu Sancto, unus es Deus, unus es Dominus: non in unius singularitate personae, sed in unius Trinitate substantiae. Quod enim de tua gloria, revelante te, credimus, hoc de Filio tuo, hoc de Spiritu Sancto, sine differentia discretionis sentimus. Ut in confessione verae, sempiternaeque Deitatis, et in personis proprietas, et in essentia unitas, et in majestate adoretur aequalitas. Quam laudant Angeli, atque Archangeli, Cherubim quoque ac Seraphim : qui non cessant clamare quotidie, una voce dicentes:

SANCTUS

Saiatatokenti, Saiatatokenti, Saiatatokenti, Sewenniio tsi iakionnhe. Karonhiakwekon onwentsiakwekon saiatanehrakwat iesasennaien karonhiake. Ronwanenton ne thare rasennakon Rawenniio ronwasennaien karonhiake.

CANON OF THE MASS

TE IGITUR, clementissime Pater, per Jesum Christum Filium tuum, Dominum nostrum, supplices rogamus ac petimus, uti accepta habeas, et benedicas haec + dona, haec + munera, haec + sancta sacrificia illibata, in primis quae tibi offerimus pro Ecclesia tua sancta Catholica: quam pacificare, custodire, adunare, et regere digneris toto orbe terrarum: una cum famulo tuo Papa nostro N., et Antistite nostro N., et omnibus orthodoxis, atque catholicae et apostolicae fidei cultoribus.

Memento, Domine, famulorum famularumque tuarum N. et N. et omnium circumstantium, quorum tibi fides cognita est, et nota devotio, pro quibus tibi offerimus, vel qui tibi offerunt hoc sacrificium laudis, pro se suisque omnibus: pro redemptione animarum suarum, pro spe salutis, et incolumitatis suae: tibique reddunt vota sua aeterno Deo, vivo et vero.

Communicantes, et memoriam venerantes, in primis gloriosae semper Virginis Mariae, Genitricis Dei et Domini nostri Jesu Christi: sed et beati Joseph ejusdem Virginis Sponsi, et beatorum Apostolorum ac Martyrum tuorum, Petri et Pauli, Andreae, Jacobi, Joannis, Thomae, Jacobi, Philippi, Bartholomaei, Matthaei, Simonis, et Thaddaei: Lini, Cleti, Clementis, Xysti, Cornelii, Cypriani, Laurentii, Chrysogoni, Joannis et Pauli, Cosmae et Damiani, et omnium Sanctorum tuorum; quorum meritis, precibusque concedas, ut in omnibus protectionis tuae muniamur auxilio. Per eundem Christum Dominum nostrum. Amen.

Hanc igitur oblationem servitutis nostrae, sed et cunctae familiae tuae quaesumus, Domine, ut placatus accipias: diesque nostros in tua pace disponas, atque ab aeterna damnatione nos eripi, et in electorum tuorum jubeas grege numerari. Per Christum Dominum nostrum. Amen.

Quam oblationem tu, Deus, in omnibus, quaesumus, bene+dictam, adscrip+tam, ra+tam, rationabilem, acceptabilemque facere digneris: ut nobis Cor+pus et San+guis fiat dilectissimi Filii tui Domini nostri Jesu Christi.

Qui pridie quam pateretur, accepit panem in sanctas ac venerabiles manus suas, et elevatis oculis in coelum ad te Deum Patrem suum omnipotentem, tibi gratias agens, bene+dixit, fregit, diditque discipulis suis, dicens: Accipite, et manducate ex hoc omnes:

HOC EST ENIM CORPUS MEUM.

Simili modo postquam coenatum est, accipiens et hunc praeclarum Calicem in sanctas ac venerabiles manus suas: item tibi gratias agens, bene+dixit, deditque discipulis suis, dicens: Accepite, et bibite ex eo omnes:

HIC EST ENIM CALIX SANGUINIS MEI, NOVI ET AETERNI TESTAMENTI: MYSTERIUM FIDEI, QUI PRO VOBIS ET PRO MULTIS EFFUNDETUR IN REMISSIONEM PECCATORUM.

Haec quotiescumque feceritis, in mei memoriam facietis.

Unde et memores, Domine, nos servi tui, sed et plebs tua sancta, ejusdem Christi Filii tui Domini nostri, tam beatae Passionis, nec non et ab inferis Resurrectionis, sed et in coelos gloriosae Ascensionis: offerimus praeclarae majestati tuae de tuis donis ac datis, hostiam + puram, hostiam + sanctam, hostiam + immaculatam, Panem + sanctum vitae aeternae, et calicem + salutis perpetuae.

Supra quae propitio ac sereno vultu respicere digneris, et accepta habere, sicuti accepta habere dignatus es munera pueri tui justi Abel, et sacrificium patriarchae nostri Abrahae, et quod tibi obtulit summus sacerdos tuus Melchisedech, sanctum sacrificium, immaculatam hostiam.

Supplices te rogamus, omnipotens Deus, jube haec perferri per manus sancti Angeli tui in sublime altare tuum, in conspectu divinae majestatis tuae: ut quotquot ex hac altaris participatione, sacrosanctum Filii tui Cor+pus, et San+guinem sumpserimus, omni benedictione coelesti et gratia repleamur. Per eumdem Christum Dominum nostrum. Amen.

Memento etiam, Domine, famulorum famularumque tuarum N. et N. qui nos praecesserunt cum signo fidei, et dormiunt in somno pacis.

Ipsis, Domine, et omnibus in Christo quiescentibus, locum refrigerii, lucis et pacis, ut indulgeas, deprecamur. Per eumdem Christum Dominum nostrum. Amen.

Nobis quoque peccatoribus famulis tuis, de multitudine miserationum tuarum sperantibus, partem aliquam et societatem donare digneris, cum tuis sanctis Apostolis et Martyribus: cum Joanne, Stephano, Matthia, Barnaba, Ignatio, Alexandro, Marcellino, Petro, Felicitate, Perpetua, Agatha, Lucia, Agnete, Caecilia, Anastasia, et omnibus Sanctis tuis: intra quorum nos consortium, non aestimator meriti sed veniae, quaesumus, largitor admitte. Per Christum Dominum nostrum.

Per quem haec omnia, Domine, semper bona creas, sancti+ficas, vivi+ficas, bene+dicis, et praestas nobis.

P: Per ip+sum, et cum ip+so, et in ip+so, est tibi Deo Patri + omnipotenti, in unitate Spiritus + Sancti, omnis honor et gloria. Per omnia saecula saeculorum.
R: Amen.

Oremus. Praeceptis salutaribus moniti, et divina institutione formati, audemus dicere:

Pater noster, qui es in coelis: sanctificetur nomen tuum: adveniat regnum tuum: fiat voluntas tua, sicut in coelo, et in terra. Panem nostrum quotidianum da nobis hodie, et dimitte nobis debita nostra, sicut et nos dimittimus debitoribus nostris. Et ne nos inducas in tentationem.

R: *Sed libera nos a malo.*

P: Amen.

Libera nos, quaesumus, Domine, ab omnibus malis praeteritis, praesentibus, et futuris: et intercedente beata et gloriosa semper Virgine Dei Genitrice Maria, cum beatis Apostolis tuis Petro et Paulo, atque Andrea, et omnibus Sanctis, + da propitius pacem in diebus nostris: ut ope misericordiae tuae adjuti, et a peccato simus semper liberi, et ab omni perturbatione securi.

Per eumdem Dominum nostrum Jesum Christum Filium tuum, Qui tecum vivit et regnat in unitate Spiritus Sancti Deus.

P. Per omnia saecula saeculorum.
R: *Amen.*
P: Pax + Domini sit + semper vobis+ cum.
R: *Et cum spiritu tuo.*

Haec commixtio et consecratio Corporis et Sanguinis Domini nostri Jesu Christi, fiat accipientibus nobis in vitam aeternam. Amen.

AGNUS DEI

Iesos Kristos seriwahtontha kariwaneren katakwentenr nisa.

Iesos Kristos seriwahtontha kariwaneren katakwentenr nisa. Iesos Kristos seriwahtontha kariwaneren takwentenr takion skennen.

Domine Jesu Christe, qui dixisti Apostolis tuis: pacem relinquo vobis, pacem meam do vobis: ne respicias peccata mea, sed fidem Ecclesiae tuae: eamque secundum voluntatem tuam, pacificare et coadunare digneris: qui vivis et regnas Deus, per omnia saecula saeculorum. Amen.

Domine Jesu Christe, Fili Dei vivi, qui ex voluntate Patris, cooperante Spiritu Sancto, per mortem tuam mundum vivificasti: libera me per hoc sacrosanctum Corpus et Sanguinem tuum ab omnibus iniquitatibus meis, et universis malis: et fac me tuis semper inhaerere mandatis, et a te numquam separari permittas. Qui cum eodem Deo Patre et Spiritu Sancto vivis et regnas Deus in saecula saeculorum. Amen.

Perceptio Corporis tui, Domine Jesu Christe, quod ego indignus sumere praesumo, non mihi proveniat in judicium et condemnationem: sed pro tua pietate prosit mihi ad tutamentum mentis et corporis, et ad medelam percipiendam. Qui vivis et regnas cum Deo Patre in unitate Spiritus Sancti Deus, per omnia saecula saeculorum. Amen.

Panem coelestem accipiam, et nomen Domini invocabo.

Domine, non sum dignus, ut intres sub tectum meum: sed tantum dic verbo, et sanabitur anima mea. (3 times)

Corpus Domini nostri Jesu Christi custodiat animam meam in vitam aeternam. Amen.

Quid retribuam Domino pro omnibus quae retribuit mihi?

Calicem salutaris accipiam, et nomen Domini invocabo. Laudans invocabo Dominum, et ab inimicis meis salvus ero.

Sanguis Domini nostri Jesu Christi custiodiat animam meam in vitam aeternam. Amen.

COMMUNION OF THE FAITHFUL

P: Ecce Agnus Dei, ecce qui tollit peccata mundi.
R: *Domine, non sum dignus, ut intres sub tectum meum: sed tantum dic verbo, et sanabitur anima mea. (3 times)*

P: Corpus Domini nostri Jesu Christi custodiat animam tuam in vitam aeternam. Amen.

SAIONKINEKWAHETSTANION

Saionkinekwahetstanion
Setewennakerate,
Oksa ionkwanisentaon
Ne Niio karonhiake.

Akoren tenhnon
Tiakotati nethone
Twariwahnirat nonwa
Ne ionkiwennakarataton

Kariwiioston
Akwa kwawenniioste
Akwekon iakwaienas
Tsinikon takwarihonniennis.

Okta tetewateronwek
Tsi rohtare ne Niio;
Iah se te kanikonhrata
Raotiohkwatokenti

O Sewennio!
Akwa tewakehtakwen
Iahte katennowentha
Ise sewenniio tsi konnhe.

Tahonenne ronwatrori
Ne sesakoskontakwen
Ne rotitokensehakwe
Nahonwaienterhane.

Rokwatton kati
Ne kento nonwentsiake
Oka nonwa iekweni
Niahta honwawenniiostake!

Akwa rawennatokenti
Ionwesen tsi rohtare
Tsi tesakoswatetennis
Sakonikonhriiostha.

Iekwenies kati
Ronwanikonhraksatha;
Ii se onkwariwa
Tsini hotatitenstetenni.

Saonkiiatewetonnion
Ne ok ne ionkiiawi
Sataionkwententaseke
Nok naetewenheie.

Tsi rawenheion
Iesos sonkwawenniio,
Tewakwekon sonkwawi
Aetionnheke karonhiake.

119

Akwekon tewanoronkwak
Tsi ionkinekwaheston;
Sasonkwanekoserawe,
Sesonkwaiatokewen.

Oksa nethone
Onkwawenk karonhiake
Sontennhoton noneshon
Nentitewariwaierite

Oksa kati, Sewenniio
Akwa waskenonwene
Tsi iahte iahonnisehon
Ne iotakssn nahoten

Kanoron kati
Iahte iahonnisehon
Onkwaterihonkohten,
Sewakatatiataksatanion

Akwa konwennaiesaton,
Konnikonhraksatakon.
Tiotkon sane seskinonkskwe,
Tekaontakwekonne.

Katstarha nonwa
Naonsaskitenrheke,
Naonkenaktotake.
Nakatsennonni karonhiake

Onen enkatewentete
Iontonweskwatha sonha;
Rawenniio raowenna
Enkianenhawe nonwa.

Iahte kakonte
Entkeriwaierite
Ne se ok iotsennonniat
Iakotatennhese niotaksen.

Onen nonwa Sewenniio
Enkatotarhoseke
Tsi iesanikonhraksatha,
Ensekswenseke notkon.

Tiotkon tsinenwe
Enkonwenniiostake
Nok enwakerhareke
Nakoniatkatho karonhiake.

ABLUTIONS

Quod ore sumpsimus, Domine, pura mente capiamus; et de munere temporali fiat nobis remedium sempiternum.

Corpus tuum, Domine, quod sumpsi, et Sanguis, quem potavi, adhaereat visceribus meis: et praesta, ut in me non remaneat scelerum macula, quem pura et sancta refecerunt sacramenta: qui vivis et regnas in saecula saeculorum. Amen.

P: Dominus vobiscum.
R: Et cum spiritu tuo.
P. Oremus.

POSTCOMMUNION

Proficiat nobis ad salutem corporis et animae, Domine Deus noster, hujus sacramenti susceptio: et sempiternae sanctae Trinitatis, ejusdemque individuae unitatis confessio. Per Dominum.

POSTCOMMUNION (Commemoration of the Sunday)

Tantis, Domine, repleti muneribus: praesta, quaesumus; ut et salutaria dona capiamus, et a tua nunquam laude cessemus. Per Dominum nostrum.
R: Amen.

DISMISSAL

P: Dominus vobiscum.
R: Et cum spiritu tuo.
P: Ite, Missa est.
R: Deo gratias.

Placeat tibi, sancta Trinitas, obsequium servitutis meae: et praesta, ut sacrificium quod oculis tuae majestatis indignus obtuli, tibi sit acceptabile, mihique, et omnibus, pro quibus illud obtuli, sit, te miserante propitiabile. Per Christum Dominum nostrum. Amen.

P: Benedicat vos omnipotens Deus, Pater + , et Filius, et Spiritus Sanctus.
R: Amen.

LAST GOSPEL

P: Dominus vobiscum.
R: Et cum spiritu tuo.
P: + Initium sancti Evangelii secundum Lucam.
R: Gloria tibi, Domine.
P: In illo tempore, dixit Jesus discipulis suis: Estote misericordes, sicut et Pater vester misericors est. Nolite judicare, et non judicabimini: nolite condemnare, et non condemnabimini. Dimittite et dimittemini. Date, et dabitur vobis: mensuram bonam, et confertam, et coagitatam, et supereffluentem dabunt

in sinum vestrum. Eadem quippe mensura, qua meni fueritis, remetietur vobis. Dicebat autem illis et similitudinem: Numquid potest caecus caecum ducere? nonne ambo in foveam cadunt? Non est discipulis super magistrum: perfectus autem omnis erit, si sit sicut magister ejus. Quid autem vides festucam in oculo fratris tui, trabem autem, quae in oculo tuo est, non consideras? Aut quomodo potes dicere fratri tuo: Frater, sine, ejiciam festucam de oculo tuo: ipse in oculo tuo trabem non videns? Hypocrita, ejice primum trabem de oculo tuo: et tunc perspicies, ut educas festucam de oculo fratris tui.
R: *Deo gratias.*

Appendix B: Other Indian Masses

Use of Kanesatake (Mohawk)

Kyrie

P. Tak8entenr Se8enniio.
R. *Tak8entenr Se8enniio.*
P. Tak8entenr Se8enniio.
P. Tak8entenr Kristos.
R. *Tak8entenr Kristos.*
P. Tak8entenr Kristos.
P. Tak8entenr Se8enniio.
R. *Tak8entenr Se8enniio.*
P. Tak8entenr Se8enniio.

Gloria

Gloria in Excelsis Deo. Nok non8entsiake skennon kenhak
nonk8e niakonikonhriio. Ise k8anentons. Ise k8anehrak8as. Ise
k8a8enniiostha. Ise k8anoronk8a. Ise tek8anoronk8anion ne
8ahonni sanehrak8at. Se8enniio iesennakeraton, iah othenon
tesanoron. Se8enniio, sonhaa Niio hiaienha Iesos Kristos.
Tetsisari8aserak8en ise, Niio hianiha. Seri8ahtontha kari8aneren,
tak8entenrane. Seri8ahtontha kari8aneren, tak8atontats
ne k8ennitha. Etho tsiteron tsi ra8eientetakon hianiha,
tak8entenrane. Tokenske saiatatokenti. Sonhaa Se8ennio. Sonhaa
iesako8anen, Iesos Kristos. Rotkon Roiatatokenti, Niio hianina,
sateietsisennaien. Ethonaia8en.

Credo

Credo in Unum Deum. Roniha iahothenon tahonoron, roson
karonhia, non8entsia, ak8ekon tsini iekens nok tsini iahteiekens.

Nok saiatat Ra8enniio Iesos Kristos, raonha Niio Rohienha. Ok sihiatatienha arekho othenon tetotierenne. Teios8atetak8a teios8atetak8ake, ak8a Niio Raonhake Niio. Tsi Roienha iahte hon8aiatison, sahniiatat Roniha, ak8ekon rote8eiennison. Ii tionk8e sonk8aniente, sonk8atsennonniatennire, karonhiake, tha8enonton. Raonniaton raieronke Rotkon Roiatatokenti, aonek8ensa Non8ari, iahte kanak8aienteri NOK ONK8E ROTONHON. Ionk8arihonni ron8aiatanentakton, Konsk8irat roterihontak8e, roronhiakenhon, ron8aiataten. Nok shotonnheton asen8atonta tsini kaiatonk8e. Karonhiake sha8enonton tsi ra8eientehtakon Roniha. Sekontentre enthoiatanehrak8atonhatie tensakoiatorete neniakonnheke nok iako8entaon, iatekakonte enhon8ennakeratse. Nok Rotkon Roiatatokenti Ra8enniio sonkionnheton; Rononhake Roniha nok Roienha thoientakon. Ne Roniha nok Roienha, satehon8ati8enniiostha, satehon8atisennaiens, ron8a8ennahnoton Rotitokensehak8e. Skentiok8at ok kentiohk8atokenti, Ratik8ekonne tehonennitiohk8arenihon. Te8akehtakon enskat ok iontatenek8ahestha, se8aterake8atha kari8aneren. 8akerhare tsi nentsiontonnhete niako8entaon. Nok iatekakonte entsiakonnheke. Ethonaia8en.

Sanctus

Saiatatokenti, Saiatatokenti, Saiatatokenti, Niio Se8enniio Sabaoth. Kananon karonhia no on8entsia saiatanerak8atsera, iesasennaien karonhiake. Ahon8anenton ne tare raosennakon Ra8enniio ahon8asennaien karonhiake.*

Agnus Dei

Iesos Kristos seri8ahtontha kari8aneren tak8entenr Se8enniio.
Iesos Kristos seri8ahtontha kari8aneren tak8entenr Se8enniio.
Iesos Kristos seri8ahtontha kari8aneren, tak8anikohnriiosthak.

Use of Lorette (Huron)

Kyrie

P. Ta8entenr Chie8endïo.
R. *Ta8entenr Chie8endïo.*
P. Ta8entenr Chie8endïo.
R. *Tahitenr Jes8s.*
P. Tahitenr Jes8s.
R. *Tahitenr Jes8s.*
P. Ta8entenr Chie8endïo.
R. *Ta8entenr Chie8endïo.*
P. Ta8entenr Chie8endïo.

Gloria

Ahon8achiendaen ˌaronhia de Dï8 a8eti nondede sken
nontha ˌenk non8e da ˌodi ˌonk8asti. Hisa ˌonchiennondiak.
Hisa sadera8as. Hisa ˌon8endiostha. Hisa ˌondoronk8a.
Hisa te ˌonnonronk8anion dei iondiak sadera8a. Chie8endïo
hesenda ˌerati taen tesatendo ronk8adik. Chie8endïo son8aena
Dï8 iena Jes8s-Keristos. Tetsi8ari8acha8en shon8aena Dï8 haïsten.
Sari8atonti ˌari8aderaï ta 8achiotat desenditha. Sari8atonti
ˌari8aderaï ta8entenrade. Tho ichitson de aien8eti ati iaïsten
ato. Lato ˌen saatato ˌenti. Shon8a Chie8endïo. Shon8ahena
esa ˌo8anen Jes8s-Keristos. D'Oki o8atato ˌenti. Dï8 haïsten
chiataietsichiendaen. Etho aia8enk.

Credo

Ri8ïastha esaatat de Dï8 hohïsten taen thadorons hochondi
ˌarondia nondede a8eti deichienk thi de taen te ˌenk. Esaatat
Ha8endïo Jes8s-Keristos haon8a Dï8 haon8aa. Chiatatiëna
asonsten tohokierennen. Tehorhathak8a tehorhathetak8a
hahon8a de Dï8. Chiho8ena taen tehon8atichiai chiahiata

127

tohisten a8eti oteïendiehiaï. Thi kion8e son8akierakie endi
shoniontharade ‚aronhia‚e eta8eti. Aondiati aheron‚e Oki
o8atato‚enti de la8enïa Marie taen te‚adak8ateri de On8e
Hoton. O8erihondi on8atanentadi. Konsk8irat hotchihontak
on8aronhia‚enti on8atonk. Onen shotonhonti achienk atontha
de thi ‚ahiaton. Laronhia‚e esa8eti aien8eti hathi Thoïsten.
Lato‚enteche thetho8adadera8atihatie tesa‚o8entoreth d'alonthe
da‚a8enhaon ate‚a‚onth ehon8en da erat. Thi d'Oki o8atato‚enti
Ha8endïo sonionhonti ahon8a de Hohïsten de Ho8ena
etha8eti. De Hohïsten de Ho8ena chiatehon8a8endiostha
chiatehon8achiendaen on8a8endadoton hotidi‚onrato‚ensk8a.
Skentiok8at otiok8ato‚enti ati8eïnen teha‚oditiok8arenion.
Therhe skat ontatendek8aestha sk8atchon8atha ‚ari8aderaï.
‚Eïarha iherhe sotonhonton aa‚a8enheon. Athe‚a‚onth
eha‚onthe. Etho aia8enk.

Sanctus

Satato‚enti. Satato‚enti. Satato‚enti Chie8endïo dodota‚ete.
Dï8 de‚aronhïa nondede satadera8as aiesachiendaen
‚aronhia‚e. Aon8aehiennondia nontare hochiendaen Tha8endïo
ahon8achiendaen‚aronhia‚e.

Agnus Dei

Jes8s Keristos sari8atonti‚anri8aderaï ta8entenr Chie8endïo.
Jes8s Keristos sari8atonti‚anri8aderaï ta8entenr Chie8endïo.
Jes8s Keristos sari8atonti‚anri8aderaï ta8adi‚onriostha.

Use of Oka (Algonquin)

Gloria

Ketcit8a8inintc icpiming Kije Manito, 8akitakamik gaie
8anaki8atc menoteedjik. Ki Kitcit8a-nikamotonimin. Ki
sakiinimin. Ki manadjiinimin. Ki kitcit8a8eniminimin. Ki
nakominimin, napitc ka kitcit8a8enindagosin. Tebenimiang
Dio 8ak8ing 8ekima8ian, Dio 8ek8isisian, kakina keta8iton.
Tebenimiang pejiko 8eosian Jezos Kristos. Tebenimian
Dio ka sasaki8inigon Dio 8eosimatc. Kaiasiama8at8a
paiatatidjik, ca8enimicinam. Kaiasiama8at8a paiatatidjik,
ca8enindamita8icinam eji pagoseniminang. O kitci niking kos
epian, ca8enimicinam; kin ma nicike ki kitcit8a8enindagos. Ki
pejiko tibenindam. Ki pejiko icpenindagos, Jezos Kristos, kiki
8enicicitc Manito Dio 8ek8isisitc o 8aseiatisi8ining. Kekona ki
ingi.

Credo

Ki tep8eton i nisopejikon Dio 8ek8isisian, kakina neta8iton,
kajiton 8ak8i aki gaie, kakina gaie naiag8ak naiag8asinok gaie.
Ki tep8eton, ki tibenim, Jezos Kristos ki pejik Dio ij oiosimatc.
Gotc kakikekamik kaiat kit ok8isisimik k'os 8atcdiomatc, 8atc
8aseiatisimatc; enditc kit int 8atc tebesimatc. Ket na ki kijiik
8atc apitenindagosimatc, epitc kijitotc kakina, anicinabek i 8i
ag8acimat8a. Kit ondjipa 8ak8ing, kit o8iia8iik 8enicicitc Manito,
kikang Mani 8iia8ing kit anicinabe8. Tcipaitikong nina8int
mi sa ka ondji nanik Pons Pinatan ki nisik; ki ning8aakas. Kit
apitcipa neso konagak, mi ekitomagak aiamie masinaigan. Mi dac
ejan 8ak8ing, kit ap k'os o kitci niking. 8ak8ing ondji apitc ki
ga pi kitcit8a tipakonak pematisidjik, ka nipodjik. Kakikekamik
ki gat okima8. Meno Manito8ian, ki tep8eton, ki pimadjii8e,
8eckisisitc 8eositc gaie 8endjipan. 8ek8isisitc 8eositc gaie ki 8itc
manadjiigom. Ki 8asenama8abanek ka nanikan kikenindangik.

129

Kitcit8a Ningot8e8anakisi8in inigok8akamikise. Nin dep8etan sikaandage8in tci kasiikatek patato8in. Nind apenimon mino apitcipa8in pon aki8ang, gaie dac kakiketa8in. Amen.

Sanctus

Kitcit8a8enindagosi, Kitcit8a8enindagosi, Kitcit8a8enindagosi Dio ka tibeniminang. Makatenindag8at ejinagositc, o manadjiigo 8ak8ing Anjeni8a gaie ondaje aking anicinabe.

Agnus Dei

Jezos Kristos, kaiasima8at8a paiatatidjik, ca8enimicinam.
Jezos Kristos, kaiasima8at8a paiatatidjik, ca8enimicinam.
Jezos Kristos, kaiasima8at8a paiatatidjik, 8anakiicinam.

Use of Old Town (Penobscot)

Kyrie

P. Zezus ketemanghelmine.
R. *Zezus ketemanghelmine.*
P. Zezus ketemanghelmine.
R. *Nixkam ketemanghelmine.*
P. Nixkam ketemanghelmine.
R. *Nixkam ketemanghelmine.*
P. Zezus ketemanghelmine.
R. *Zezus ketemanghelmine.*
P. Zezus ketemanghelmine.

Gloria

Aghim ketahkamimook uleyoltidjik kessisseyoltidjik
kemamptchimulpena, kulimulpena, ketalasomulpena,
ktchitamitehelmulpena, ndwetchi moywalleku, Ktchi Sangmanwi
tehelmokussian anixkam wesangmanmieku Spemook eyan
anixkam wekussian messiu kegus nittawittawan. Nixkamieku
Zezus nilon n'dwetchi uyusowelsiasa anixkam wemiktankussian,
ayamata wata uskitchinwak uneyotiwal ketemanghelmine;
ayamata wata uskitchinwak uneyotiwal, wehulitehelmine
utinahkanaghepittawan kemiktangus wehulistawine kill
kutokkahiu Sangmanwian, kill kutokkahiu kessisseyane,
kill kutokkahiu ketchitamitehelmokussian Zezu-kli tedebiu
Sangmanwi tehelmokussit wetchi uleyt nixkamwit. Te eleyt.

Credo

Wekussit messiu kegus nittawittaku Spemook kisittankusan,
nesaktam wewitahansine Zesus Nixkam pesekual kwissal
negman kesangmanmeno wetchi uleyt Nixkam mawelasabanill
Malie Nanxkwet eyaptchiutch alasozin Ponse Pilate + negman

Zesus amekane klotchieutahats, nepohotnas pusquenass, elanmkamikook elihesse nesughenighiskak amena waunsiness Spemkamikook eyeku utinahkanaghepittawall umiktankusall, messiu kegus nittawittolit yaptchiutch mtchitch nantsi yalasoman nepkopanik aweskitchinwidjik tanne kes elwekasoltilit nesaktam wewitahansine wetchi uleyt Nixkam; sangmanwi Klassian Catholicam kessisseyultidjik eli pesekwitit noneyotinwalmeniak uminwhiniatch messiu, messiu uskitchinwak eli uyusittit ayaptchiutch uleyottwak spemkamikook epultidjik. Te eleyt.

Sanctus

Kessisseyan, Kessisseyan, Kessisseyan, wesangmanmiek yalasoman Anzeliak uskitchinuak. Ketchi Sangmanwi tehelmokusit spemook ak ktahkamikook tchibatook ulimesk. Nixkam, Zezus, Spemook utchi nantsi ulasouyane.

Agnus Dei

Zezus aymata uskitchinwak uneyotiwal. K'temanguelmine.
Zezus aymata uskitchinwak uneyotiwal. K'temanguelmine.
Zezus aymata uskitchinwak uneyotiwal. K'milgonena Kbesgwinena.

Appendix C:
Proposed Adaptation of the Indian Mass to the *Novus Ordo Missæ*

The current rubrics of the *Novus Ordo Missæ* explicitly allow for the substitution of the Mass Propers with suitable hymns at the Entrance, Preparation of the Gifts, and Communion, so it is possible to adapt the new Mass to more closely follow the traditional Indian Mass. Below is an outline of the current Mass, and I have indicated in bold where texts from the Indian Mass could be sung in the native language. Naturally, the specific texts used will vary according to the mission.

INTRODUCTORY RITES

Entrance Song: **Introit of the day**
Greeting
Rite of Blessing and Sprinking: **Asperges**
Penitential Rite
Kyrie: **Kyrie**
Gloria: **Gloria**
Opening Prayer

LITURGY OF THE WORD

First Reading
Responsorial Psalm: **Gradual***
Second Reading
Alleluia or Gospel Acclamation: **Alleluia** (where this exists)
Gospel
Homily
Profession of Faith
General Intercessions

Preparation of the Altar and Gifts: **Offertory hymn**
Prayer over the Gifts
Preface
Holy, Holy, Holy: **Sanctus**
Eucharistic Prayer
Lord's Prayer
Sign of Peace
Breaking of the Bread: **Agnus Dei**
Private Preparation of the Priest
Communion: **Communion hymn**
Period of Silence or Song of Praise
Prayer after Communion
Greeting
Blessing
Dismissal

---

* The Latin Gradual can be sung in place of the Responsorial Psalm, but the *General Instruction on the Roman Missal* does not permit the use of hymns in its place (GIRM #61). Thus, hymns that substitute for the Gradual in the Indian Masses cannot be used in the *Novus Ordo Missae*. If no native-language Graduals are available, then the Responsorial Psalm is to be sung.

Appendix D:
Liturgical Calendar for Kanesatake/Oka

The following calendar is taken from the *Tsiatak Nihononwe*, which seems to be the only paroissien with a full liturgical calendar. I have left all the names of the feasts and saints in French, as most of them are sufficiently evident. A few of the most common labels and abbreviations are as follows:

abbé = abbot
archange = archangel
évêque *or* év. = bishop
doct. = doctor [of the Church]
diacre = deacon
mart. *or* m. = martyr
N.D. = Our Lady
pape = Pope
pr. *or* p. = priest
religieux = religious
roi = king
v. = virgin.
veuve = widow

The month names were originally in French and Mohawk—I have translated the French portion and left the Mohawk as in the original.

January / Tsiotorko8a

1 LA CIRCONCISION.
2 St. Macaire, évêque.
3 Ste. Geneviève, v.
4 St. Fite, évêque.
5 St. Emilienne, v.
6 L'EPIPHANIE.
7 St. Lucien, pr. m.
8 St. Gudule, religieux.
9 St. Julien, Ste. Basilisse.
10 St. Guillaume, évêque.
11 St. Hygin, p. m.
12 Ste. Césarie, veuve.
13 Ste. Hermyle.
14 St. Hilaire, évêque.
15 St. Paul, prem. ermite.
16 St. Marcel, p. m.
17 St. Antoine, abbé.
18 La Chaire de St. Pierre à Rome.
19 St. Sulpice.
20 SS. Fabien et Sébastien.
21 St. Meinrad, Ste, Agnes.
22 St. Vincent, diacre.
23 St. Ildefonse, évêque
24 St. Timothée, év. m.
25 Conversion de St. Paul
26 St. Polycarpe, év. m.
27 St. Jean Chryst., doct. év.
28 St. Amédée, évêque.
29 St. François de Sales, év.
30 Ste. Martine, v. m.
31 St. Pierre Nolasque.

Le 2e Dim. après l'Epiphanie, fête du St. Nom de Jésus

February / Enniska

1 St. Ignace, év. et m.
2 LA PURIFICATION
3 St. Blaise, év. et m.
4 St. Maire, éveque.
5 Ste. Agathe, v. m.
6 Ste. Dorothée, v. m.
7 St. Romuald, abbé
8 St. Jean de Matha.
9 Ste. Apollonie, v. m.
10 Ste. Scholastique, v.
11 St. Adolphe
12 Ste. Eulalie, v. m.
13 Ste. Catherine de Ricci
14 St. Valentin, p. m.
15 { St. Faustin, m.
     Ste. Georgie, v.
16 Ste. Julie.
17 St. Fintan, abbé
18 St. Siméon, év. et m.
19 St. Boniface, éveque.
20 St. Eucher, éveque.
21 Stes. Eléonore, Vitaline et Verda
22 La Chaire de St. Pierre à Antioch
23 Ste. Romaine.
24 St. Mathias.
25 St. Césaire, médecin.
26 St. Nestor.
27 { St. Léandre,
     Ste. Honorine, v. et m.
28 St. Sérapion

March / Ennisko8a	April / Oneratokha
1 St. Albin	1 St. Hugues
2 Ste. Blandine	2 St. François de Paule
3 Ste. Cunégonde	3 St. Richard
4 St. Casimir	4 St. Isidore
5 St. Théophile	5 Ste. Irene
6 St. Fridolin	6 St. Sixte
7 St. Thomas d'Aquin	7 St. Hégésippe
8 St. Philémon	8 St. Amance, St. Albert
9 Ste. Françoise	9 Ste. Marie Cléophé
10 40 martyrs	10 La B. Mechtide
11 St. Constantin, m.	11 St. Léon, pape, doct.
12 St. Grégoire-le-Grand	12 St. Jules
13 Ste. Modeste	13 St. Herménégilde
14 St. Mathilde	14 SS. Tiburce et Valér
15 St. Longin	15 Ste. Anastasie
16 St. Héribert	16 St. Lambert, St. Martial
17 Ste. Gertrude	17 St. Anicet, St. Rodolphe
18 St. Alexandre	18 St. Eleuthère
19 St. Joseph	19 St. Léon, pape
20 St. Joachim	20 St. Théotime
21 St. Benoît	21 Anselme, év. doct.
22 le B. Nicolas de Flue	22 SS Sotère et Caïus
23 Ste. Théodosie	23 St. Georges, mart.
24 Ste. Hildelite	24 St. Fidèle
25 L'Annonciation	25 St. Marc, évangéliste
26 St. Emmanuel	26 St. Marcellin
27 St. Jean l'ermite	27 Ste. Madeleine de Pazzi
28 St. Gontran	28 SS. Vitule et Valérie
29 St. Victorin	29 St. Robert, abbé
30 St. Jean Climaque	30 Ste. Catherine de Sienne
31 St. Benjamin	*Le 2e Dim. après Paques, fête du Patronage de St. Joseph*

May / Oneratako8a

1 Ss. Philippe et Jacques
2 St. Athanase
3 Invent. de la Ste. Croix
4 Ste. Monique, veuve
5 St. Ange, m.
6 St. Jean Porte Latine
7 St. Stanislas, év. m.
8 Apparit. de St. Michel
9 St. Béat.
10 St. Antonin
11 St. Mamert
12 St. Gengulphe
13 St. Servais
14 Ste. Justine
15 St. Honoré
16 St. Jean Népomucène
17 St. Paschal
18 St. Alfred
19 St. Yve
20 St. Bernardin
21 St. Félix de Cantalice
22 Ste. Yolande
23 St. Désiré
24 Ste. Jeanne
25 St. Urbain
26 St. Philippe de Néri
27 St. Prisque
28 St. Emile
29 St. Maxime
30 St. Ferdinand
31 Ste. Pétronille

*Le 3e Dim après Pâques, fête de la
Ste. Famille.*

June / Oiariha

1 St. Fortuné
2 St. Erasme
3 Ste. Clotilde, reine
4 St. François Caracciolo
5 St. Boniface
6 St. Claude
7 St. Norbert
8 St. Médard
9 St. Félicien
10 St. Marguerite, reine
11 St. Barnabé
12 St. Antonine
13 St. Antoine de Padoue
14 St. Basile
15 St. Bernard de Menthon
16 SS. Ferréol et Ferjeux
17 St. Rainier
18 St. Léonce
19 SS. Gervais et Protais
20 St. Sylvère
21 St. Louis de Gonzague
22 St. Paulin
23 St. Ediltrude
24 Nat. de St. Jean-Bte.
25 St. Guillaume
26 SS. Jean et Paul
27 St. Ladislas
28 *Jeûne.* St. Irénée
29 SS. PIERRE et PAUL
30 Comm. de St. Paul

*Le vendredi après l'octave du St.
Sacrement, fête du Sacré Coeur
de Jésus*

July / Oiariko8a

1 St. Théobald
2 LA VISITATION
3 St. Héliodore
4 St. Udalric
5 St. Agathon
6 Ste. Lucie
7 St. Félix
8 Ste. Elisabeth de Port.
9 St. Véronique
10 Ste. Félicité et ses 7 fils
11 St. Pie, pape, m.
12 St. Jean-Gualbert
13 St. Eugène
14 St. Bonaventure
15 St. Henri
16 N.-D. de Mont-Carmel
17 St. Alexis
18 St. Frédéric
19 St. Vincent de Paul
20 Ste. Marguerite
21 Ste. Praxède
22 Ste. Marie-Madeleine
23 St. Apollinaire
24 St. Christine, v. m.
25 St. Jacques
26 St. Anne
27 Ste. Nathalie
28 SS. Victor et Innocent
29 Ste. Marthe
30 St. Abdon
31 St. Ignace de Loyola

le 1er Dim. de juillet, fête du Précieux Sang

August / Seskeha

1 St. Pierre-aux-Liens
2 St. Alphonse de Liguori
3 Découv. du corps de St. Etienne
4 St. Dominique
5 N.-D. des Neiges
6 Transfiguration
7 St. Gaétan
8 Ste. Cyriaque
9 St. Romain
10 St. Laurent
11 St. Tiburce
12 Ste. Claire
13 St. Hippolyte
14 *Jeûne.* St. Eusèbe
15 L'ASSOMPTION
16 St. Hyacinthe
17 St. Anastase
18 Ste. Hélène
19 St. Louis
20 St. Bernard
21 Ste. Jeanne Fr. de Ch.
22 St. Philibert
23 St. Adolphe
24 St. Barthélemi
25 St. Louis, roi de France
26 St. Adrien
27 St. Césaire, év.
28 St. Augustin
29 Décoll. de St. Jean-Bte.
30 Ste. Rose
31 St. Raymond

Le Dim. après l'oct. de l'Assompt. fête du St. Cœur de Marie.

September / Seskekowa

1 St. Gilles
2 St. Lazare
3 Ste. Dorothée
4 Ste. Rosalie
5 St. Laurent-Justinien
6 St. Magnus
7 St. Cloud
8 LA NATIVITÉ
9 St. Gorgon
10 St. Nicolas de Tolentin
11 St. Félix et Ste. Régule
12 St. Valérien
13 St. Aimé
14 Exalt. de la Ste. Croix
15 St. Nicodeme
16 St. Corneille
17 Ste. Hildegarde
18 St. Thomas de Villen.
19 St. Janvier
20 St. Eustache
21 St. Mathieu
22 St. Maurice
23 St. Lin, Ste. Thècle
24 St. Gérard
25 St. Firmin, Ste. Aurélie
26 SS. Côme et Damien
27 St. Florentin
28 St. Venceslas
29 St. Michel, archange
30 St. Jérôme

*Le Dim. dans l'oct. de la Nat., fête
    du St. Nom de Marie.*

Le 3e Dim., fête des 7 Douleurs.

Octobre / Kentenha

1 St. Rémi, év.
2 SS. Anges Gardiens
3 St. Candide
4 St. François d'Assise
5 St. Placide
6 St. Bruno
7 Ste. Justine
8 Ste. Brigitte
9 St. Denis
10 St. François de Borgia
11 Ste. Placidie
12 St. Maximilien
13 St. Edouard, roi
14 St. Calixte, pape, m.
15 Ste. Thérése
16 St. Gall, abbé
17 Ste. Hedwige
18 St. Luc
19 St. Pierre d'Alcantara
20 St. Jean de Canty
21 Ste. Ursule
22 Ste. Alodie
23 St. Jean Capistran
24 St. Raphaël, archange
25 SS. Crépin et Crispinien
26 St. Evariste, pape, m.
27 St. Frumence
28 St. Simon et St. Jude
29 St. Narcisse
30 Ste. Zénobie
31 *Jeûne.* St. Quentin

Le 1er Dim., fête du Rosaire

Novembre / Kentenko8a

1 LA TOUSSAINT
2 Comm. des Fid. Trép.
3 St. Hubert
4 St. Charles Borromée
5 St. Guiraud
6 St. Léonard
7 St. Ernest
8 St. Dieudonné
9 St. Théodore
10 St. André Avellin
11 St. Martin de Tours
12 St. Martin, p. m.
13 St. Stanislas Kostka
14 Ste. Vénérande
15 St. Léopold
16 St. Edmond
17 St. Grégoire, thaumat.
18 St. Odon
19 Ste. Elisabeth de Hong.
20 St. Félix de Valois
21 Présentation de N.-D.
22 Ste. Cécile
23 St. Clément, pape, m.
24 St. Chrysogone, m.
25 Ste. Catherine
26 St. Conrad
27 St. Colomban
28 St. Sosthène
29 St. Saturnin
30 St. André

Decembre / Tsiotorha

1 St. Eloi
2 Ste. Bibiane
3 St. François-Xavier
4 Ste. Barbe, v. m.
5 Ste. Crispine, m.
6 St. Nicolas
7 St. Ambroise, év. et d.
8 IMMACULÉE CONC.
9 Ste. Léocadie
10 St. Melchiade
11 St. Damase
12 Ste. Judith
13 Ste. Luce
14 St. Agricole, m.
15 St. Célien
16 Ste. Adélaïde
17 St. Florian
18 St. Gratien
19 St. Némèse
20 St. Zenon
21 St. Thomas
22 St. Flavien
23 Ste. Anastasie
24 *Jeûne.* St. Delphin.
25 NOEL
26 St. ETIENNE, prem. m.
27 St. JEAN
28 Le Saints Innocents
29 St. Thomas de Cantor
30 St. Sabin
31 St. Sylvestre

Appendix E: The Anglican Liturgy in the Algonquian and Iroquoian Missions

Protestant missionaries also produced prayer and hymn books in native languages, but these, expectedly, did not give a great deal of attention to liturgy, even though a few quasi-liturgical formulas can be found in them, as for instance in the Delaware litanies produced by the Moravians (Zeisberger and Luckenbach 1847).

The closest Protestant equivalents to the Catholic Indian Masses are seen in the Anglican Order for Holy Communion in the *Book of Common Prayer*. Translations of the English and American liturgies were prepared for the Mohawk, Oneida, Minsi Delaware , Ojibwe and Cree (Muss-Arnolt 1913).

It is worth noting that—quite aside from the liturgical differences between the Roman Missal and the Book of Common Prayer—the Anglican missions took a quite different linguistic approach. Whereas the Catholic liturgies only had a limited vernacularization for the portions assigned to the choir, the Anglican ones are entirely in the vernacular start to finish, though a few of the books do indeed give the English on a facing page.

Yet even among Anglicans, it seems that there remained some tension between those who favored the retention of traditional English over the Indian vernaculars, as noted within the preface of a Mohawk edition of 1842:

> Objections have been made to any attempt to translate a work like the Book of Common Prayer into a language so rude and uncultivated as the Indian, into which it is deemed impracticable to effect any satisfactory version. To remove from the Indians any motive to learn the English language, or to furnish therewith any excuse for remaining content with their own, has been held by some inexpedient.
>
> But the Company hopes to find from this partial interchange of languages a tendency to a different

result, that a mutual desire and a mutual facility may be promoted for the acquisition of each, and that it may contribute to the accommodation, both of future teachers and learners. In the mean time, without regard to the merits or demerits of the Indian language, it seems an imperative duty to omit no opportunity of assisting those invited to join in acts of devotion, speedily and effectually to understand the language in which those acts are performed, and it is certainly desirable to remove any extraneous difficulty, that might, from the use of a strange idiom, arise in untutored minds to comprehending and satisfactorily adopting some parts of this much valued formulary. The Indian Catechumens in North America ought to be placed in this respect at least on an equal footing with their fellow Christians on the eastern side of the Atlantic. (Nelles 1842)

The two different approaches of total and partial translation reproduce, in their own way, the arguments that have come to the fore since the Second Vatican Council about the respective values of a liturgical language and the vernacular.

Bibliography

Anonymous. [1755]. *Livre des prières, cantiques, et himnes en langue hyroquois telles qu'on se sent maintenant à la Mission du Lac des Deux Montagnes...* Original in Laval University, Séminaire de Québec (Fonds du Séminaire), Archives no, 309, 1848. Copy at the American Philosophical Society, Microfilm 254(4:4), Freeman and Smith #1838.

Béchard, Henri, S.J. 1976. *The Original Caughnawaga Indians.* Montreal:International Publishers' Representatives (Canada) Ltd.

Boudreau, Gérald C. 1996. "The *Nujjinen* of the Mi'kmaq People and the Construction of their Chapel at Bear River, Nova Scotia" *Nova Scotia Historical Review*, Vol. 16:1, pp. 7-20.

Buckenmeyer, Jacob. 2007. "Tekakwitha attendees urged to follow in footsteps of Blessed Kateri," *Catholic News Service*, July 2, 2007.

Cabrol, Dom Fernand. 1934. *The Mass of the Western Rites.* St. Louis, MO:B. Herder.

Campeau, Lucien. 1989. *Les Grandes Épreuves (1638–1640).* Monumenta Novae Franciae, Vol. 4. Montrèal:les Èditions Bellarmin.

Catlin, George. 1866. *Illustrations of the Manners, Customs, and Condition of the North American Indians with Letters and Notes... .* London:Henry G. Bohn.

Charlevoix, P. F. X de. 1900. *History and General Description of New France. Translated from the original edition and edited, with notes, by Dr. John Gilmary Shea.* New York:Francis P. Harper.

Chauchetière, Claude. 1887. *La Vie de la B. Catherine Tegakoüita, dite a present La Saincte Sauvagesse.* Manate[Manhattan]:Cramoisy Press.

Company = Company Magazine online. 1996. *The Word of God.* http://www.companysj.com/v141/contents.html, accessed June 26, 2008.

Cuoq, Jean André. 1865. *Tsiatak Nihonon8entsiake onk8e on8e akoiatonsera....* Tiohtiake [Montreal] tehoristorarakon John Lovell.

ibid. 1882. *Lexique de la Langue Iroquoise avec notes et appendices.* Montréal:J Chapleau & Fils.

ibid. 1893. *Ocki Mino Masinaigans.* Moniang[Montréal]: Tak8abikickote endatc J. M. Valois.

Devine, E.J. 1922. *Historic Caughnawaga.* Montreal:Messenger Press.

Dictionary of Canadian Biography. 1988. Toronto:University of Toronto Press.

Dubois, Paul-André. 1997. "Hymn-Singing in the Vernacular in the Missions of New France and the Conquest of Indigenous Languages: an Unknown Link" *Recherches Amerindiennes au Quebec* 27, 2.

ibid. 2002. "Innovation et langue vulgaire: Les chants mobiles du Propre de la Messe dans les missions de Nouvelle-France", *L'espace missionnaire, lieu d'innovations et de rencontres interculturelles,* sous la direction de Gilles Routhier et Frédéric Laugrand, Actes du colloque de l'Association francophone œcuménique de missiologie du Centre de recherches et d'échanges sur la diffusion et l'inculturation du christianisme et du Centre Vincent Lebbe,

Québec, 23-27 août 2001, Paris, Karthala, 2002, p. 141–156.

Durocher, Flavien. 1847. *Aiamie Kushkushkutu Mishinaigan*. Ka iaokingants, nte Opishtikoiats [Quebec]:nte etat William Neilson.

Dwight, Sereno Edwards, ed. 1822. *Memoirs of the Rev. David Brainerd; Missionary to the Indians on the Borders of New-York, New-Jersey, and Pennsylvania: Chiefly Taken from his own Diary*. New Haven: S. Converse.

Franks, C. E. S. 2002. "In search of the savage sauvage: an Exploration into North America's political cultures." *American Review of Canadian Studies* Vol. 32, no. 4:547–581.

Higginson, J. Vincent. 1954. "Hymnody in the American Indian Missions" *The Papers of the Hymn Society*, XVIII.

Kaiatonsera Teieriwakwatha. 1890. Tiohtiake:Tehonaristorarakon E. Senekar nok Roienha.

Korolevsky, Cyril. 1957. *Living Languages in Catholic Worship: A Historical Inquiry*. London, New York: Longmans, Green.

L'Opinion Publique. 1870. "Procession à Caughnawaga le jour de la fête-dieu", Vol. 1, no. 27, pp. 213 (July 7, 1870).

Langevin, Edmond. 1874. *Notice biographique sur François de Laval de Montmorency 1er évêque de Québec: suivie de quarante-une lettres et de notes historiques sur le chapitre de la cathédrale*. Montreal:Lovell.

Lebret, Louis Marie. 1866. *Niina Aiamie masinaigan ou recueil de prieres et de cantiques a l'usage des sauvages de Temiscaming, d'Abbitibi, du Grand Lac, de Mata8an, et du Fort William*. Moniang [Montreal]: tak8abikickote endatc John Lovell.

147

Maurault, J[oseph] A[nselme]. 1866. *Histoire des Abenakis depuis 1605 jusqu'à nos jours.* [Sorel, Quebec?]:l'Atelier Typographique de la "Gazette de Sorel".

McNaspy, Clement. 1947. "Iroquois Challenge: Chant in Approved Vernacular." *Orate Fratres* 322–327.

Miller, J. R. 1996. *Shingwauk's Vision: A History of Native Residential Schools.* Toronto:University of Toronto Press.

Miller, Wick R. 1996. "The Ethnography of Speaking", in Ives Goddard, ed., *The Handbook of North American Indians, volume 17: Languages.* pp. 222–243. Washington D.C.:Smithsonian Institution.

Muss-Arnolt, William. 1913. *The Book of Common Prayer among the Nations of the World.* London:Society for Promoting Christian Knowledge.

Nelles, Rev. Abraham and John Hill. 1842. *The Book of Common Prayer, according to the use of the Church of England, translated into the Mohawk language...* Hamilton:Ruthven's Book and Job Office, &c., King Street.

Neilson, J.L. Hubert. 1908. *Facsimile of Pere Marquette's Illinois Prayer Book.* Quebec:Quebec Literary and Historical Society.

Pilling, James Constantine. 1888. *Bibliography of the Iroquoian Languages.* Washington D.C.:Government Printing Office.

Pilling, James Constantine. 1891. *Bibliography of the Algonquian Languages.* Washington D.C.:Government Printing Office.

Positio = *The Positio of the Historical Section of the Sacred Congregation of Rites on the Introduction of the Cause for Beatification and*

Canonization and on the Virtues of the Servant of God Katherine Tekakwitha, The Lily of the Mohawks. 1940. New York: Fordham University Press.

Powers, Rt. Rev. Msgr. James M., ed. 1957. *The Martyrs of the United States of America: Manuscript of Preliminary Studies.* Easton, PA:Commission for the Cause of Canonization of the Martys of the United States.

Ratzinger, Joseph Cardinal. 2000. *The Spirit of the Liturgy.* San Francisco:Ignatius press.

Saint-Vallier, Jean-Baptiste de la Croix de Chevrières de. 1856 [1688]. *Estat présent de l'Église et de la colonie française dans la Nouvelle-France.* Quebec.

Sasseville, J. 1887. "An Illinois Manuscript of Fathers Allouez and Marquette," pp. 334–338 in *U.S. Catholic Historical Magazine,* vol. 1. New York:United Catholic Historical Society.

Sioui, Georges E. 2000. *Huron-Wendat:The Heritage of the Circle.* Vancouver and Toronto:UBC Press.

Tooker, Elisabeth. 1978. "The League of the Iroquois: its History, Politics, and Ritual." *The Handbook of North American Indians volume 15: Northeast.* pp. 418–441. Washington D.C.:Smithsonian Institution.

USCCB. 2002. *Native American Catholics at the Millennium: A Report on a Survey by the United States Conference of Catholic Bishops Ad Hoc Committee on Native American Catholics.* United States Conference of Catholic Bishops:Washington, D.C.

Valigny, R. P. Pacifique de. 1912. *Alasotmamgeoel: Paroissien Micmac/Prayer-Book in Micmac.* Restigouche:Ste Anne de Ristigouche, P.Q.

Various artists. 2001. *Wli-nuelewi: Mi'kmaw Christmas Music*. CD. Executive Producers Atlantic Canada's First Nation Help Desk and Mi'kmaw Kina'matnewey. Sydney, Nova Scotia.

Vecsey, Christopher. 1997. *The Paths of Kateri's Kin*. Notre Dame, Indiana:University of Notre Dame Press.

Verwyst, Chrysostom. 1886. *Missionary Labors of Fathers Marquette, Menard and Allouez, in the Lake Superior Region*. Milwaukee and Chicago:Hoffmann Bros.

ibid. 1900. *Life and Labors of Rt. Rev. Frederic Baraga, First Bishop of Marquette, Mich*. Milwaukee:M. H. Wiltzius & Co.

Vetromile, Eugene. 1866. *The Abnakis and their history, or Historical Notices on the Aborigines of Acadia*. New York:James B. Kirker.

ibid. 1858a. *Indian Good Book*. New York:Edwatd Dunigan & Brother (James B. Kirker).

ibid. 1858b. *Ahiamihewintuhangan:the prayer song*. New York: Edwatd Dunigan & Brother (James B. Kirker).

Vintimille, Caroli Gaspar Guillelmi de. 1736. *Breviarium Parisiense*. Paris.

Wampum, John B. and H. C. Hogg. 1886. *Morning and Evening Prayer, the Administration of the Sacraments, and certain other Rites and Ceremonies of the Church of England; Together with Hymns*. London: Society for promoting Christian knowledge.

Zeisberger, David, and A. Luckenbach. 1847. *A collection of hymns, for the use of the Delaware Christian Indians, of the missions of the United Brethren, in North America*. Bethelehem, PA:J. and W. Held.

Index

C

D

Also available in the Massinahigan Series

Brief History of King Philip's War 1675-1677,
    by George M. Bodge (1891)

Sketches of Ancient History of the Six Nations,
    by David Cusick (1825)

The Country of the Neutrals,
    by James H. Coyne (1895)

Annual Narrative of the History of the Sault,
    by Claude Chauchetiere (1686)

For more information on this series, see our website at:
http://www.evolpub.com/Massinahigan/BAENA.html